sharing the SPIRIT

for and by
cheerleaders, dancers, & coaches

Sue Ann Kawecki

National Library of Canada Cataloguing in Publication Data

Main entry under title:

   Sharing the spirit : for and by cheerleaders, dancers and coaches

ISBN 1-55369-131-8

   1. Sports—Literary collections. 2. Canadian literature (English)—21st century. I. Kawecki, Sue Ann, 1971-

LB3635.S46 2001   C810.8'0355   C2001-904182-9

TRAFFORD

This book was published *on-demand* in cooperation with Trafford Publishing.
On-demand publishing is a unique process and service of making a book available for retail sale to the public taking advantage of on-demand manufacturing and Internet marketing. **On-demand publishing** includes promotions, retail sales, manufacturing, order fulfilment, accounting and collecting royalties on behalf of the author.

Suite 6E, 2333 Government St., Victoria, B.C. V8T 4P4, CANADA
Phone·   250-383-6864   Toll-free   1-888-232-4444 (Canada & US)
Fax   250-383-6804   E-mail   sales@trafford.com
Web site   www.trafford.com   TRAFFORD PUBLISHING IS A DIVISION OF TRAFFORD HOLDINGS LTD.
Trafford Catalogue #01-0533   www.trafford.com/robots/01-0533.html

10   9   8   7   6   5   4   3   2   1

table of contents

team

believe

spirit

coach

hit it

just dance

teammates

success

let's hear it
for the boy

making it big

center stage

acknowledgments

Thank God for the Internet! Over the past two years, my trusty computers and the World Wide Web have made the progress of this book possible. The Internet has allowed the creation of a global support network for cheerleaders and dancers that cannot be paralleled. There truly is a "sharing of the spirit" online!

Through contacts made with various webmasters of numerous websites, I was able to spread the word that I was looking for stories that reflected the passion and the heart that resides within every cheerleader, dancer, and spirit coach. The request was forwarded from e-mail to e-mail worldwide. The response was incredible. And voila, here is the end result!

Although I decided to go with self-publication, this does not in any way infer that I did all the work! This compilation would not have been achievable without the hundreds of writers who shared their experiences with me. Although only a fraction of those, 133 stories (to be exact), were selected, I would like to thank each and every single person who took the time to expose their hearts on paper!

There are many people and organizations to whom I would like to extend my gratitude. Their excitement and support inspired me to finish this project. Each and every one served as my own personal cheerleader! A special heartfelt thanks goes out to the following:

The Maine East Demon Squad—all members, past and present (especially my Mohicans—Tanvi, Katie, Karolina and Nikisha)—you have been there through and through. I matured with the four of you and am a wiser and better person because of our friendships. You may be gone but will never be forgotten! My love for the sport is daily refueled each and every time I go to practice and interact with all of my girls. I couldn't be more blessed! Kelly Clifton, my first captain ever and now my fellow coach. You define the very word, 'spirit'. Shine on, my original golden girl. And my head captain Gina G.—you make me proud every day. I couldn't have asked for a better captain and friend.

The Bobrich sisters, Barbara and Melsa, for supporting me and always being there with your words of wisdom. For the better part of two decades, Barb and her team have motivated me, first as a dancer and now as a coach.

The various Dance/Drill Associations who posted my requests. Especially Halftime Illinois, Illinois Drill Team Association, and DTDA (Drill Team Directors of America). Melissa Interrante of DTDA, editor of INSIGHTS, do you know how many stories I received with your name on the referral? Your dedication to dance is to be commended!

The editors of *Dance Spirit*, *In Motion*, and *American Cheerleader* magazines for plugging the book and supporting it from the beginning! Julie Davis published my first article ever…I will never forget you! Lynn, ex-editor of *In Motion*, and owner of Spirit Direct, your upbeat attitude and your editing skills have helped me tremendously as a writer!

The Cheerlist. Cheerlist is a listserve of cheerleaders and coaches from throughout the world who are there to lend an ear and offer advice to any cheerleader or coach in need. Besides the numerous submissions sent from Cheerlist members, I would like to thank "THE LIST" for your enthusiasm and your advice on everything—from tryouts to tattooes! A special thanks to Pam Headridge, the acclaimed coach of Oak Harbor, who was always willing to send me a needed picture for an article or this book! Generation All-Stars…check out your pic!

The numerous spirit companies for also spreading the word and their support in this endeavor. UDA/UCA, NDA/NCA, Just For Kix, UPA, Jamz Camps, COA, Mid-American Pom, Badgerette, Cheer LTD…your avid support shows that your companies aren't in this for the money but for the kids and the SPIRIT!

Bob Kiralfy and BCA—our dedicated and astute counterpart across the ocean. His words of wisdom often soothed my mind when things with my team were rough! Be sure to check out his bio for info on him and his British site.

The coaches, dancers, and cheerleaders of all the pro sport dance/cheer teams—I don't think anyone was more excited than you! Jay Howarth, a prominent leader in the Spirit Industry, for her just as valuable, but different view on things. Thank you for our conversation—I remember it to this very day!

Joyce Pennington and ADTS for their support. Thank you for spreading the word with your newsletter. Leslie Goettsch, the mastermind behind DanceCheer.net, the original support network for dancers and cheerleaders alike. Jenni Einsvold of *Cheers and More*, her innovation and dedication to cheer is incredible. Suite 101.com's, About.com's and CheerHome.com's webmasters for their written support for *STS*.

Erin Cullen, my graphic artist and fellow coach. Thanks for fitting right in the scheme of things. With the book and with the team, I am ecstatic to have you!

Patty Killian, my brave colleague abroad. You go girl!

Susan Havens, formerly of National Spirit, you definitely set my sights on greatness. Thank you for your faith in the project.

My alma mater dance team, the 1985-1989 Lisle Lionettes from Lisle, Illinois. The wonderful experiences and memories that we created and shared together fueled my passion to continue on with coaching and writing. Especially Karen Rees—the best teammate, captain and a friend one could ever want in life! Smile, sparkle, shine!

I'd also like to bring special attention to some other websites that impressed and encouraged me—Cheerleader Land, G.C's Comprehensive List of Cheerleading on the Web, edanz.com, and The College and University Cheerleading Directory.

There are many more people that I have encountered on this wonderful journey that I have failed to recognize. If you are amongst those, just remember that the success of this book would have been unattainable without you!

Lastly, I'd like to thank my family. Life has been full of some pretty deep potholes along the way, and I've had several people who have repeatedly helped me up, brushed me off, and sent me on my merry way. My little brother Jimmy—my constant companion in life's early adventures and beyond. I wouldn't be alive without you—need I say more? My sister Tasya, my role model of strength and bravery. You are on your way to greatness. I hope I have been life's cheerleader for you as much as you have been mine. My auntie Corinne—I thank God every day for you. Besides the fact that I want to be just like you, you are my rock. My husband, Billy—the quintessential jock. We make the perfect pair, do we not? I am always here to cheer you on. And my Jami and Jason, the two reasons for my existence and my utter happiness. I will forever be by your sides. And finally, my daddy in heaven. It's always been for you.

introduction

From the moment that we first took the floor, I knew right then and there that I was a goner. Yup—I had gone over the deep end—hook, line and sinker.

It's not as if I were some prima donna or something…all eyes riveted to me as I leaped and spun across the floor. Back then, as a freshman, I was lucky enough if I could double-step to the beat! Rather, I was swept away by the passion…my own and that of those around me, dancing with me, performing with me, living with and through me.

I don't even remember if we placed at the camp competition that summer. But to me, it didn't really matter. Through dance, I had found my niche. As a team, we had created a harmony, a field of positive energy that radiated from us as we danced towards a common goal.

That's what it's all about—harmony. And that's what motivated me through four years of high school, and now as a coach of a high school dance team. Of course, I can't say that success on the competition mat isn't of crucial importance! Winning a trophy for something that you love to do is definitely a bonus! Being looked upon as a serious athlete, more so, takes the cake! But creating a communal balance amongst teammates tops it all.

As precision dancers and cheerleaders, we all have been there and done that. And at the core of every cheerleader's and dancer's heart, we all know that the creation of such harmony is the reason why we continue on, even when school administrators, parents and newspapers give us a bad rap.

"Activity or sport?" they rant on and on. "Airheads with short skirts and revealing tops," they say to describe us. "It doesn't take an athlete to jump around and smile," they argue.

My reply…*"Whatever!"*

Sure, it stings when people snub something that I have dedicated my life to. It hurts even more when my team is looked over by the budget committee year after year! It absolutely makes my blood boil when I hear someone describe what my girls do as an "activity".

But, essentially, it doesn't truly matter what those who haven't been touched by the Spirit think. We have persevered for 100 years without their support, and we will continue to do so—as long as we support each other.

And that's what this book, ***Sharing the Spirit—for and by cheerleaders, dancers, and coaches*** is all about. It's not about what the feature writer from Sports Illustrated thinks about cheerleading; it's not about Title IX; it's not about being included in the football program. It doesn't even boil down to being called an activity rather than a sport (though for the record, I lean extremely towards the "sport" contingent). ***Sharing the Spirit*** is about supporting one another, applauding each other's efforts, and nurturing that special harmony…that spirit…that lives within us all.

Sue Ann Kawecki

team

Excellence takes togetherness

There is No "I" in TEAM

"Teamwork is the ability to work together toward a common vision…it is less we and more WE!"

Welcome to my world of one

It's me, myself and I.

I know you've come to see me cheer

Watch me as I fly.

Coach says it's best to be a team

I can't imagine why.

I'm so much better than the rest.

That's me up in the sky.

Our halftime show is really hard

I need to be up front.

The other kids just can't compare

Watch me as I stunt.

I am the best, I am first-rate

It's plain for all to see.

I'm #1, I am a star

The cheer revolves around me.

It happened oh so suddenly

My stunt began to fall.

My teammates knew just what to do

They saved me after all.

My spotter held me steady

The bases stayed in tight.

They prevented a disaster

On that important night.

I now value my teammates

I know we're all first-rate.

It's everyone together

Being a part of a team is great.

No longer do I think of me

It takes all to be supreme

This is why my coaches say

"There is no "I" in TEAM."

-Author Unknown
-Submitted by Katie Robison

Items a Dancer Should Pack

***You may have the greatest bunch of individual stars in the world, but if they don't play together, the club won't be worth a dime.* ~Babe Ruth**

It was the summer before my senior year. Four years on poms and never had I EVER attended a camp. By taking conveniently planned trips, I had always managed to avoid going; however this year it was to be different. Being that I was going into my second year as captain, my coach and my teammates encouraged me to attend a camp designed to challenge even the most experienced of dancers.

My coach's sister directed our rival team, the other top squad in the area. But for some unknown reason the two sisters always persuaded us in attending camps and competitions together as "sister squads". I was about as interested in spending 5 days at the upcoming camp in Louisville, Kentucky with four strangers, our competitors even, as I was in undergoing triple bi-pass surgery!

Needless to say, I was deeply concerned that the six-hour car ride to Kentucky would be an exercise in torture. It wasn't long before my suspicions were confirmed. Along with the four strangers and the two coaches, the coaches' three stinky dogs joined us on our cross-country venture in a van with no air conditioning! To top it off, I was on a completely different wavelength than my fellow campers—whenever I felt like napping they were screaming and whenever I wanted to talk they were sleeping. Just when I thought my level of agitation had reached a record high my coach bust out the pamphlet for the camp...

"Wake Up-7:00am." The words rang in my head. Wake up? This was summer, a time to relax and sleep! She continued as I listened with terror.

"Warm up-7:30... 1st class-8:00, 2nd Class-10:00, Lunch-Noon, 3rd Class-12:30..."

What? A thirty-minute lunch break after dancing an entire morning and then they expected us to continue like we didn't need to digest the food?

"Workshop-2:30, 4th Class-4:30..." The classes continued with no breaks until 9:00PM. Yup, that's right, non-stop dancing from 7:30 in the morning until 9:00 at night with one lousy half hour break for lunch. Kentucky was not sounding hospitable.

At that point all I could think about was jumping out of the stifling rented Suburban and hitchhiking with a dirty trucker back to my home where I could sleep in, eat, and relax to my heart's content. Nothing in the world could prepare me for the next line of news...

"List of Items Dancers Should Pack," Coach read.

We all listened intently, each wondering why we hadn't been told what we needed to bring until we were cutting through Indiana. "...Dance Attire, Alarm Clock, Linens..."

"Linens?" shrieked Heather, the outspoken one amongst us. "We need linens?"

"That's what it says here. You girls are sleeping in a dorm; it's not like a hotel where they do your laundry, ya know," Coach Bobrich chuckled.

We didn't have linens. We didn't even have towels.   Yup, this was going to be a fun, fun time. It was as if I had died and had "Lousy Pom" engraved on my tombstone!

At best one would suppose that I would soon after quit the team and try every form of therapy to relieve myself of this horrible tragedy. But I was wrong. The situation from hell was transformed into the best five days of my pom career.

The bonding was intense. Initially we marched into the peppy dance camp as five individuals and encountered unified teams of twenty. They intimidated us with their impressive uniforms and perfect hair. We, who hadn't even showered or brushed our hair! To assimilate, we had to unite as a squad and dominate the concept of pep. As dancers for halftime shows, we had left the pep to the cheerleaders.

Leaving camp five days later, I came away with a new dance style, increased endurance and a sense of spirit... but most importantly the experience taught me what it meant to be part of a team. I never could have survived at that camp without those girls, and they couldn't have survived without me.

Together we brainstormed for linen solutions, we choreographed dances, we practiced, and we breathed. Together, we became discouraged, cried and pulled muscles. But together we overcame every obstacle before us. As individuals, we won many honors but more importantly as a "team" we left a mark on all the other squads.

I learned so much in so little time and it will affect me forever.

Sunney Kohlhoss

I Wish...

Alone we can do so little; together we can do so much.
~Helen Keller

A few years back my youth cheerleading team competed at a league competition hosted by a local school. Artwork and papers that the grammar school children had completed decorated the school's hallways.

One of the hallways featured an "I wish..." display. Each child had written about the one thing that he truly wanted. Most of the items wished for were the usual--"puppy", "video games", and "bicycle". But one specific wish caught my team's attention: "I wish I had my own bed to sleep in." We looked at that one for a long time and suddenly *our* wish for a first place trophy had become meaningless!

With that one sentence, we were quickly brought back down to reality! Here we were, so nervous about doing well, and trying to capture first place, while this little girl just wanted her very own bed—something that we all took for granted. It was all we could talk about for the rest of the day. We knew we had to do something to grant her her wish.

The following morning, a talk with the school's principal answered all of our questions. Who was this girl? Why was she without a bed? Both the girl and her little sister were either sleeping in their parents' bed or on the floor because individual beds could not be afforded.

A cheerleader's father was so moved, he himself purchased a set of twin beds for the girls. All the cheerleaders chipped in and bought two sets of sheets, pillows and a comforter for each girl. Shortly after dropping them off at the girls' school, we received a phone call from the principal. She told us that the two little girls were so happy. They could not believe that total strangers would do this for them.

We really felt good about doing this and since then have yearly attempted to do a service project for our community.

Karen Topping

The Big Day

"Think big, believe big, act big, and the results will be big."

Today's the big day...

Time to put to the test

To see which team,

Is truly the best.

Ready for our chance to arrive,

Teeming with spirit, brimming with pride,

As they call our names out loud,

Standing tall, and standing proud.

Ever ready to show our best.

More than ready to outdo the rest.

We've waited for this moment,

Now it's finally here.

Come on team,

Let's show them how to cheer!

Amie Crace

Drive To Succeed

To succeed...You need to find something to hold on to, something to motivate you, something to inspire you. - Tony Dorsett

To cheer, to compete, to win…

All of these things must come from within.

The drive, determination, the power to succeed-

It resides within our spirit…it's all that we need.

Practicing hard, day after day

Never giving up

When things don't go quite our way.

It's what makes us winners,

Causes our faces to beam

When it all comes together

As we work as a team.

Together we accomplish all that we desire

Our dreams are our wings

That take us much higher

So hold our heads high and let's do our best

We should be proud of ourselves

Above all the rest.

Crystal Martin

Passion

Passion is in all great searches and is necessary to all creative endeavors.
~Eugene W. Smith

In anticipation we await the beat that causes our hearts to pound. The spectators' silence is unbearable. Our thumping hearts and our silent prayers are deafening in comparison. But all we can do is hold our pose and wait for the first beat of music to fill the gym. This is our only chance to do what we came here to do and to prove what we came here to prove.

As the music begins, a thousand thoughts flow through my head. I am suddenly hit with the realization that this is my last dance with the team. This is my last dance and last chance to win a state title. As a team, we want it, and we deserve it...

The progress we have made in the past few years is astonishing. Three short years ago, I was the only one with any dance experience. My three years as a leader has left me mature and confident but I cannot deny that I too have learned much from my team. Although I am the captain, I am not the best dancer, but nevertheless I have learned to become very proud of those who dance better than I do. I have also learned that sometimes the key to loving something is understanding it. Aside from the fights, the disappointments, and pettiness, when we looked within, we ultimately discovered what it took to be a great team.

This is my dance, the dance that I choreographed. It is an amazing experience to see a dance go from visualization to reality. But the difficult thing is getting everyone to share the vision, to feel the emotions, and to live the dance. Yet that is very thing that we strive for, the feat that makes it worth enduring countless hours of practice and bodily fatigue, the feat that allows us to overlook and overcome the lack of school support.

As the music comes to a stop and our routine concludes, I look around at my teammates, and I can tell that we are sharing the same incredible sentiment. Running off the gym floor for the very last time, I realize that we have all gained so much from being a part of this team. We have all gained patience, responsibility, trust, devotion, and love. We no longer dance just for ourselves or for our audience, but most importantly, we dance for each other.   We all share a passion, a passion to dance.   But we, as a team are fortunate, we share this passion, not only as teammates but also as friends.

Natalie Minns

Pyramid

"When does a cheerleader become an athlete? During a stunt like this..."

Gathered outside the coliseum, Staff prepared the next day's material. Cheers, dances, chants and … pyramids! Ha! The staff moaned collectively, as they all shared a feeling of dread when it came to that particular class. But as Head Instructor Angela had said, there was no getting out of teaching Pyramids! So they reluctantly got up and got on the ball. Pyramid, after pyramid, after pyramid…

Need I tell you how exhausted the cheer staff was? After having taught classes from seven in the morning until nine in the evening, the instructors defined "bone-tired". Needless to say, as far as pyramids went, not everything was going as planned! Still, the grumpy, pessimistic and bitter staff continued to build. Pyramid, after pyramid, after pyramid…

There was one pyramid in particular that was causing the staff a lot of grief. In fact, it was one that they always struggled with, regardless of exhaustion. But the lack of teamwork and patience on this specific evening made it even worse. Staff greatly feared attempting it the next day.

Well, after a good night's rest, the staff made it through the following day's classes. Jumps, cheers, and stunts… next on the agenda—the dreaded Pyramids! Being instructors, experts at "pulling out" skills when necessary, you would think they would face the challenge head on. Not! They were unusually nervous.

Bravely, they formed a line in front of the entire camp. Words of fear and worry were shared. In the distance, Angela, Head Instructor Extraordinaire, looked on…silently cheering them on, as only a head cheer instructor can. Still, they all felt that that they would not hit the infamous pyramid.

Who would have known though? Someone, somehow, suddenly got the biggest shot of optimism coursing through his veins. It quickly became contagious. Words of encouragement were shared.   From one end of the line to the other raced quiet prayers of hitting it. From that end back to the other raced threats of getting fired if they didn't!

All of a sudden, WE, the staff, went wild! The campers thought us crazy. Laughter, exclamations, hand slapping, and back patting dominated as we attempted to build the horrid pyramid. All the commotion for one stinkin' pyramid! Anyway, as we settled ourselves down, we built it…perfect, flawless, an unbelievable sight of achievement!

Of course, we looked to Angela for approval. And again, as only a head cheer instructor could, she beamed from ear to ear. That smile and look in her eyes said it all. We, as a staff, had just been reminded, while some of us had just been taught, how significant the human mind and heart can be. As a team, we pulled it together, reached and achieved a common goal. In this case, it was a not-so-simple pyramid—but the lesson could be applied in so many other ways, in so many aspects of life.

Often we forget to appreciate the others in our lives. Those people that love us and that will support us in our endeavors. At this certain time in my life, the NCA staff made up those important people. The staff, a unique group of talented people, was my "summer family".

We often think that we can do anything and everything on our own. But sometimes we need to remind ourselves to slow down, to swallow our pride, and to ask for help. Even the slightest word of encouragement can take you through tumultuous times. Everyone needs to "lean" on someone sometime in their lives…not just in Pyramids class! Why not? The celebration of success is so much more fun when shared with others!

Shannon Cajayon O'Toole

A Drill Team Prayer

Coming together is a beginning, staying together is progress, and working together is success. **~Henry Ford**

Lord let us give thanks for teammates, coaches, family and friends

For their love and support during good times and bad.

This has been a year to celebrate success, talent, creativity and unforgettable memories.

As a team we can be proud to know that we were respectful,

Honest, and hardworking. But most of all we believed in ourselves

And did our very best with the Lord's unselfish guidance.

May God watch over and guide next year's team and give them

The ability to develop the same high standards and ideals

That our team has shared this year.

May you always trust in God,

Believe in yourself and dare to dream!

In the Lord's name, we pray, amen.

Melissa Spata

Picking Up the Pieces

You win only if you aren't afraid to lose. ~Rocky Aoki

An excited glow emanates from my mentor's eyes as she anxiously awaits our performance. In my coach's face, I see hours upon hours of frustration and hard work poured into making this one moment a success. All of the practice will have been worth it if only to make this one face beam with pride and satisfaction at a job well done.

The crowd in the bleachers before me melts into one buzzing mass of energy and, for a second, I forget to breathe. It is this moment for which we have worked two years. Two years of conditioning, stretching, and learning choreography, through sprained ankles, sore knees, and pulled hamstrings.

The rest of my pompon team is behind me, and they want this as badly as I do. I'm not sure what my sisters are thinking. Some are, no doubt, nervous. Some are ready. Some are terrified. But as for me, I feel alive. It is during these rare moments, when anticipation and excitement overwhelm me and produce an exhilarating adrenaline rush, that I am really living.

Competition is the stuff of life. It sends me to a realm where I feel as though I'm dreaming, but the dream is more vivid than reality. And as the music washes over any remaining connection to fear and nervousness, I forget that we are being judged. I forget that this one performance determines if we continue on to the State Championship or if it marks the end of a season.

Moves, that in practice shoot throbbing pain into my joints, feel like pure bliss. My badly bruised knees and weak ankles feel as if they could dance on forever. It's a peculiar sensation--the crowd disappears, and all I see are colors and music and light. "Seeing the music" is a phenomenon that happens when the rhythm and choreography overtake all of my senses, so that nothing exists but the performance. This heaven flashes by in an instant.

As we exit the floor, my elevated mood begins to fade. What if our best wasn't good enough? Maybe that wasn't our best. Maybe I could have been sharper. What if someone made a mistake? What if our timing was off? A sea of doubt and uncertainty floods into my mind. And as the next few minutes are dedicated to rehashing every possible weakness in our performance, my teammates' faces--smiling with everything in them only a moment earlier--become uncertain and dejected.

I make my way back to the rows of bleachers designated for our parents and fans by the blue and gold apparel that is their distinguishing feature. Greeted by a chorus of praise and enthusiasm, I begin to feel slightly more optimistic about our chance of qualifying for State in March. Hopefully, the judges thought the performance was as phenomenal as our fans did, but somehow, I doubt it.

Where is Missy? Where's our coach? She'll tell it like it is. Not necessarily with her words, but with her eyes. I find her amidst asthma inhalers and ankle tapes, offering deliberately objective comments about the performance. "Overall, it was a nice job. I am proud of you guys."

Her eyes, however, communicate to me uncertainty, a doubt, a fear that the season may have just ended when the music had stopped. Coupled with those emotions is a hope that forces me to try and convince myself of the best. I am certain that our work was not in vain. I am confident that when you put everything you have into something, the only possible result is success. Reassuring myself with these affirmations is unfortunately only moderately effective.

A few hours later, after the rest of the teams have competed, comes the moment of truth. Everyone scrambles onto the gym floor to hear what teams will be competitors at State and which ones will be spectators. My teammates and I, seated in an irregular circle, join pinky fingers as we agonize through the infinite list of class B qualifiers. Next, it is our turn. Farwell, Ithaca, Nouvel. School after school is called, and it seems as though Valley Lutheran is not on the list. Amanda, sitting to my left, says, "It's in alphabetical order," and I breathe a sigh of relief; that's why they haven't announced us yet. And then, when I least expect it, I hear the announcer, "Congratulations to all of the state qualifiers. This concludes the morning competition." Across the circle from me sits my coach. Her face is frozen with shock. Stunned eyes refuse to blink as she chokes back emotions of devastation and disappointment.

We failed.

Failure is an experience common to everyone at some point in life. Often it happens when one slacks off or doesn't want to reach the goal badly enough. Usually, people give up before the real work starts--they aren't willing to make the sacrifices to achieve excellence. These were possible obstacles that we had already recognized and had overcome. We had the dream. We set the goal. We put in the work. And we failed... I failed. My best was not good enough. Or at least what I had thought was my best wasn't good enough. There has never been a point in my life when I've thought less of myself than I did that day. And yet, there has never been an experience that taught me more. A thousand successes before that had not taught me to understand and come to grips with my own shortcomings. They had not taught me that life doesn't always work out the way you plan, but that you still have to pick up the pieces and work with what you've got.

Later that day, when other teams were out celebrating their achievements, we were stretching and conditioning, in preparation for the next season. If we had been denied the agonizing experience of seeing our mentor defeated and let down, we would not have vowed to never see it again. We would not have gotten up early to run before school started. We would not have dreamed about and hungered for success with the tenacity that engulfed our lives for the next two years. What we had thought was the best work of our lives indeed was not. Rather, it was an important stepping stone in developing a mentality that would produce the best work of my life in the future. Failure instilled in us a fierce desire that resulted in future success. Without it, my team would have been satisfied for that one day. We would have patted ourselves on the backs and smiled at our coach with a cheaper, blander version of accomplishment.

Each of us will be faced with a decision when failure inevitably happens. We can either allow that failure to mark the end of a noble pursuit, or we can harness the passionate emotions that it invokes. Utilizing devastation and disappointment to drive us on, we can strive for and attain greater successes than we could have ever originally envisioned.

The real success came two years later just after we had won the State Championship. My coach's eyes gleamed with pride. Striving so adamantly toward our goal of qualifying for State, we demanded excellence. And in the process of producing excellence in our performances, winning took care of itself. Because of our focus and our dream, even the State Championship was within our grasp. In the afterglow, a friend of mine asked, "When did you know for sure you had won?" Not knowing he meant at what time during the day, I responded, "My sophomore year, after we failed to qualify for State. I decided then that we would win."

It was not until then that I understood the power of failure. It can either make you quit or help you win.

Choose.

Failure will present itself; that is out of our control. It is only up to you what you will make of that failure.

Megan Lambart

For Kacee

Do what you can, with what you have, where you are . ~**Theodore Roosevelt**

Several years ago, I coached a 6th grade and under All-Star cheer squad. One evening prior to our Friday departure for Nationals, one of the climbers, Kacee, was consistently having trouble dismounting from a pyramid. I, as well as rest of the team, was concerned that the bases might not get there in time to catch her.

Finally, after a whole evening practice, we felt confident with the dismount. To insure her safety, we ran the drill one more time to make sure that we had gotten it down just right. However, as she dismounted, the bases got sidetracked and failed to catch her. Down she fell…landing on the gym floor, hitting her head extremely hard.

Fortunately, Kacee's mother was in attendance that night. Although our practices are usually closed to parents, her mother was helping me with some last minute preparations for Nationals. Her mom immediately rushed her to the hospital. After checking her out, the hospital sent her home with a clean bill of health.

Two days later, at the airport, it was obvious that Kacee was not physically well. Always so full of spirit and excitement, she now lay lifelessly in her mother's arms. According to the doctors at the hospital who had re-checked her after the tragic fall, Kacee merely had a virus. As we flew to Atlanta, she began to dry-heave. As soon as we landed, the paramedics evaluated her once again. As we boarded our flight to Orlando, Kacee was instead rushed to Atlanta's Children's Hospital.

Upon the team's and my arrival at the hotel, I received a message that things were not good for Kacee. She had been grossly misdiagnosed twice. Apparently Kacee had suffered a horrible concussion. She was bleeding internally behind her eye and her brain was dangerously swelling.

After taking the time to calm down and evaluate our choices, I visited with the Nationals' staff to inform them of our situation and to ask for their advice. I was told that we would have falls counted against us if Kacee's pyramids did not go up.

Not being able to make this difficult decision alone, I implored the squad to choose from the following three options: 1) Do not perform at all and enjoy our time at Disney World; 2) Do the routine as is without Kacee's pyramids going up; or 3)

Immediately rework the routine with a new climber. Hence, there would be no time for us to visit the amusement park.

To my surprise, but without hesitation or disappointment, the entire team opted to rework the routine. "For Kacee," they chanted.

Up until this point I was secretly hoping that they would choose not to perform so that I could be at Kacee's side. The crisis had seriously depleted all my energy and enthusiasm. But after looking at their faces and into their eyes, and after feeling their determination, I could not help but to embrace their fire.

We spent the next several hours reworking the routine, the evening teaching the new formations and the last morning prior to Nationals preparing the new climber. The team worked hard to pull it together and to overcome this incredible setback. And overcome it they did.

Our team finished 8th in the nation.

Miraculously Kacee pulled through too. The last day of our visit, she joined us in our venture at Disney World. Her teammates pushed her around in a wheelchair and to top it off, they presented her with the trophy that they had won in her honor. A year later, Kacee recovered 100%.

The team has recovered too…but not without recounting its blessings. We begin each practice and performance with a prayer. Each teammate has a strong understanding that our abilities are gifts from God. If we are willing to listen to His will and have faith in His plan, the best will always follow.

Many things happened during Kacee's crisis that proved that God was truly with us during this difficult time…

Each climber had a letter sewn into the inseam of her skirt so that when the pyramid would go up, they could lift their skirts to display a word. The night before we left for Nationals, Kacee had inadvertently left her skirt with me. Having packed it in my suitcase, I was able to give the skirt to Kacee's substitute. The skirt was a perfect fit.

The young girl who stood in for Kacee had never climbed prior to Nationals. In two hours, she learned and beautifully performed a liberty, a scorpion and a full down.

Although it was extremely unfortunate that Kacee's concussion had been misdiagnosed in Shreveport, the misdiagnosis made it possible for her to be treated later at one of America's best hospitals for children and the best physicians it had to offer.

We were given exactly enough time to accomplish what needed to be accomplished to perform well.

There are many things that I am required to teach as an All-Star coach; however I cannot teach "faith, heart and desire." It is up to the individual to possess such qualities. This amazing story shows what we can accomplish through heart, desire and a willingness to follow God's will.

Susan Wiman

Hit It!!

There can only be one state of mind as you approach any profound test; total concentration, a spirit of togetherness, and strength. **~Pat Riley**

It was a given that our team would annually compete at least once. Naturally, ever year, we highly aspired to qualify for Nationals, but alas, we inevitably always fell short. Each loss was more disappointing than the last, but we persistently returned, in hopes of clinching that National bid.

When we started practicing for camp the summer before my sophomore year, I was hit with the revelation that we were destined for greatness. Not only because I was a new and enthusiastic captain, but also because six of the twelve girls on our team were returning from the year before. Our spirit was soaring and our energy was contagious. We proved our superiority by bringing home the Spirit Stick, a Superior Trophy, and three chosen Camp All-Stars.

A month after camp we began practicing for competition. I knew that if we were ever going to make Nationals it was going to be that very year. With that thought in mind, the other captain, our three coaches and I together choreographed an awesome routine.

Throughout our routine, the crowd encouragement and spirit rode at a constant high and the sure-fire stunts were guaranteed to awe the crowd. But as the days went by, we failed to hit several choreographed stunts and planned formations. Discouraged, the entire team became irritated and hostile not only to the routine, but to each other as well.

Naturally, as a captain, I was hurt and I felt as if I had failed. It had been my responsibility to make this routine, and it just was not working. I quietly carried this burden on my shoulders and in my heart. I chose not to share my feelings with the rest of the team. I hoped that we could salvage the routine after all and that it would lead us to victory.

Three days before competition we held our last practice. Knowing that time was against us, we were extremely anxious and the tension ran high. With forty minutes left, our coach asked us to perform the routine as we would at competition.

It did not go well. Formations were out of line and stunts dropped like flies. When we finished, fury flew freely. Girls started pointing fingers and putting blame on each other. I just plopped down and cried.

After twenty seconds of havoc, our coached yelled, "HEY! SIT DOWN NOW!"

We immediately sat down in a circle, tears streaming down our faces. Coach glared down at us all, for quite some time, in pure silence. She exclaimed, "Girls, look what this is doing to all of you! You are an awesome team, we all know that, but if this is what happens when you perform a two-minute routine on a stage in front of some judges, it is just not worth going. I do not think that you girls should go to this competition on Sunday."

We were all devastated that she had actually said that, though about half of us agreed that we were not ready. So we sat there and discussed what to do. After about ten minutes, our coach agreed to let us perform the routine one more time. If we hit it, we would compete. If we didn't, we would stay home.

We got up, stood in formation, and shouted "HIT IT!" And we did exactly that. Every stunt was hit and every voice was heard.   It was perfect. The last words, " THE BEST ", rang out and that was what we were.   Immediately we cried, screamed and jumped all over one another joyously.

We had learned something about ourselves that we had somehow forgotten along the way. We had rediscovered that we could do it. The twelve of us, working together as one family, could do anything.

We didn't place that Sunday, but nevertheless we still had reached a significant goal. Who cared if we were not going to Nationals? We had done it; we had hit it. And in my opinion, we had hit it pretty darn good that day.

Victoria Balun

Never Give Up

"There are no limitations to ones' dreams. We can never fly in the sense of birds, but we can always soar to great heights."

During a rainy day in March of 1997 one of the biggest moments in a team's existence was taking place. We were competing for a national title. Everything was going as we had hoped it would.

We were executing our routine as we had only dreamed. The pyramids went up solid. We could not hear the crowd cheering, but we knew we were putting on a show that they would always remember. The months and countless hours of practice and sacrifice were paying off. Reaching our line-ups for our fifteen-person, synchronized tumbling sequence, I psyched myself up for the gravity-defying feat I was about to undertake. One could hear everyone land perfectly in sync ... flawlessly ... almost. Landing on my ankle incorrectly I could feel nothing but pain...

Although cheerleading epitomizes team athletics, the individual is responsible for doing her part to keep the machine running smoothly. Thus, I could not let myself down, and most importantly, I would not let down my team. I finished the routine with not a whimper, but a grandiose smile.

I performed for the love of the sport and my teammates. Taking home the second place trophy far outweighed the two weeks I painfully spent on crutches, and I will never forget the proud sensation of accomplishment I felt, having taken hold of a dream and refusing to let go.

Jennifer E. Tomon

We're Doing This For God

The nice thing about teamwork is you always have others on your side.
~Margaret Carty

I tie my shoes and change my clothes

Then the music starts to play.

I glance around as people gather;

It's my routine for the day.

The chatter starts and faces drop

As we begin to jog.

Still we do our best and give our all

Because we're doing this for God.

We fall in place and start our "groove";

This is the best part.

We review the old and start the new,

Giving it all from our hearts.

None of us are perfect

At sometime we each fall.

That's when our teamwork shows its face

Each time one of us calls.

Sometimes it's hard to make it

When so much else is going on.

Still we do our best and give our all

Because we are doing this for God.

As the years begin to pass

The memories seem to add.

We're thankful for the time together

And all the fun we've had.

So when we look back on this,

We should have nothing to regret.

And thank God for what he's given us

And the people that we've met.

Stacy Westerman

The Future

A team is a team is a team... ~Dan Devine

As we step onto the floor we are finally one.

There are no friends, no enemies, only a team.

We think of the ones who aren't out here with us,

But who are still part of the circle that cannot be broken.

The problems of the past are behind us;

Only the future of the squad lies before.

Our faces are glowing; our smiles are bright

And all the nervousness is forgotten.

Instead in its place is the excitement of being where we are.

We are finally one.

There are no friends, no enemies, only a team.

As competition draws close, remember these words and live by them.

Let us show not only to others, but also to ourselves

The unified team that we have become.

Author Unknown

What I Would Give

Sweat plus sacrifice equals success. ~Charlie Finley

What I would give to be first in the state…
I'd give up my free time 'cause I know how to wait
For that excellent feeling that we're doing great
At our encore performance after we have won State.

I'd get bruised. I'd get broken, for one little chance
To be out there pomming that classic-style dance,
To be out there pomming, so crisp and so clean
With all of my sisters, my pommers, my team.

I'd give up my license. I'd impound my car.
I'd walk farther than farther than farther than far.
Of course, once I got there, I'd always be late!
But that would be worth it to be first in the state.

I'd take all my possessions and burn them to ashes,
And amidst the sparks and the smoke and the flashes,
I'd not worry one bit if I knew after State
That I could go buy some more to celebrate…

That we'd done it. We'd won! After all of that work
Sacrifices paid off with significant perks:
A trophy, a banner, a little respect.
And then I'd sit down to take time to reflect.

There was only one thing I would never have traded.
I pondered, and after a while I stated,
"What I would **not** give to be first in the state

Is something so precious, so grand, and so great.

That championship trophy and its coveted gleam

Could never replace my pommers, my team."

Megan Lambart

believe

In order to succeed, we must first believe
that we can." ~ Michael Korda

Maine East High School, Coed Cheerleaders

Believe

Belief consists in accepting the affirmations of the soul.
~Ralph Waldo Emerson

Life consists of countless dreams

Whose attainment is never as far off as it seems.

You should always set yourself a high goal.

And reach for it with your heart and soul.

Every day you are surrounded by tests…

Have you worked hard? Have you done your best?

You can eventually have all the success that you want,

If you know what to do and learn to what not.

Every one is special in his or her own way,

You show this in what you do and say every day.

If you believe in yourself, then you will succeed.

Believing in yourself is a definite need.

If you always do what you believe to be right,

Life will take off like a bird in flight.

All your dreams can definitely come true.

If you believe in all that you do.

You should always, always reach for the stars,

And your life will improve by far…

Life consists of countless dreams,

Whose attainment is never as far off as it seems!

Laura Mitchell

Cheerleaders are Dumb!

Sports do not build character. They reveal it. ~ John Wooden

What you are about to read may seem like a story that has been told a million times over. However the events in this story have changed my life, and that is what makes it so special...

Growing up, I was the quintessential tomboy. Unfortunately, I had a much older sister who would torture me by dressing me up, fixing my hair, and putting make-up on me. Too young to protest, I was forced to "mascot" for her cheerleading squad.

Once grade school hit though, I tried my hardest NOT to be a girl. I played football with the best and the toughest of the boys. My friend Steph and I completely rejected femininity. We even formed a club that only the "tough" girls could join.

By the time I hit junior high, I had slowly grown out of this stage. I even kind of enjoyed being a girl! The one thing I vowed that I would never do, though, was to become a cheerleader. Cheerleaders stood for everything that I had ever been against...I mean, come on, they acted ditzy, were perpetually perky, wore skirts that were too short and looked like total idiots when dancing to some cheery song with those big grins pasted on their faces! NO WAY. That was not for me. I was into grunge and other "bad girl" things. "Cheerleaders are dumb," was my motto.

Then I became friends with Rae Ann, a girl who was totally into being a cheerleader and who was a good one at that. For my entire sophomore year, she bugged me about trying out for the team. I vigorously refused time and time again-- at first because I thought cheerleading was stupid, and then later because I lacked the confidence to actually go for it. I had been overweight most of my life and had suffered from low self-esteem. But Rae Ann would not give up on me and finally, I caved. I thought that at the very least it would be a riot to attend tryouts to make fun of everyone else.

Then something happened...I actually began to enjoy what I was supposedly being forced to do! Clinics were a blast. I got acquainted with people that I had always dismissed as shallow, and they were a lot of fun to be around. I also realized that I wasn't half bad at cheering! It instilled a confidence in me that I didn't know that I could ever possess. I was so nervous at tryouts, though, that I was convinced that I had flubbed the whole thing. Nothing could quite match that feeling I got when my name was announced as one of the six 1998-1999 cheerleaders at our annual athletic banquet!

Two years later I have become a different person in every aspect in my life. I thank cheerleading for that! As corny as it may sound, I feel invincible once I put on my cheer uniform. Sure, I've had my share of trying moments—squad fights, irate fans, stereotypes, and a broken ankle a mere week before UCA All Star tryouts—but somewhere along the way I became a very strong individual.

People still laugh at me and say, "Cheerleaders are dumb. I would never become one."

I just smile and reply, "Don't be so sure about that!"

Nicci Boots

Don't Be Afraid to Dance Alone

***Great dancers are not great because of their technique; they are great because of their passion.* ~Martha Graham**

I began my illustrious dance career lip-syncing and dancing to Martika and Debbie Gibson in my living room.   No, it was not Britney Spears and Christina Aguilera that inspired me, but the early MMC'ers. During those formative years, budding dancers like myself expressed their passion though cheerleading. I, however, was determined to attend a summer camp that was geared towards dance teams.

I tried my darndest to recruit fellow classmates. I desperately needed someone to hold my hand as I tread the waters of trained dancers. I successfully secured a new transfer student. Eager to take advantage of every opportunity, we planned and prepared for the home showcase and skit night. We were scared and excited over the whole thing. I guess the whole prospect was even scarier for her than me... a week before the big event, she backed out!

My hard-earned money and effort were not to go to waste. A week later, I walked into the Just For Kix camp ready to perform. In a large gym, adorned in a homemade pink lycra outfit accessorized with blue and white Nike shoes, I danced solo. The many hours I spent practicing were reflected by my performance. I shined. I was rewarded with a standing ovation, not for my single turn or bent-legged kick but for the passion and gumption to go out on the floor by myself.

Self-esteem bolstered, I danced my way through two more camps, several Orange Bowl appearances, and choreography competitions. After the completion of high school, I thought that there would be no more opportunities open to me due to my lack of technical training. So without any expectations, I tried out for the local college dance team. No training, but again passion and potential landed me a position on the up-and-coming team. Now we, the Minnesota State University-Mankato dance team, are two-time national champs!

I have realized my goals and am dancing at a level that I could only have dreamed about during those long hours that I practiced diligently in my living room way back when. I plan to dance for many years to come.

No, I have not reached the stardom that some of those Mickey Mouse Club members did. But my attitude, ambition and hard work have definitely paid off! The point is that everyone should take on every opportunity with smiles in their hearts and on their faces. If I didn't dance by myself I couldn't have danced at all. Dance has made me the person I am today.

Angela Mickelson

I Am

I can; therefore I am. ~Simone Weil

I am dedicated

I am organized

I am reliable

I am creative

I am dependable

I am responsible

I am energetic

I am determined…

I am ready.

Erin Cullen

Forever Faithful

Happiness can exist only in acceptance. ~Denis De Rougamont

As a child, I was extremely shy. I thought I was alone in the world. I didn't have many friends, and so I felt that there was something wrong with me. At school, the boys mercilessly teased me, and I resigned myself to the depressing fact this was how life was always going to be.

Growing up, I was aware of the many rumors that circulated about cheerleaders. Many of those rumors I thought were true.   Cheerleaders were all supposedly blonde, and I thought that they all sat around, twirling their coiffed hair around their index fingers, and chewed gum. As I got older, I watch movies that only affirmed these views. Cheerleaders always seemed to be jumping around in the background, chanting pointless words, and waving impossibly huge poms. I didn't need to convince myself to know that the sport simply wasn't for me, so I easily steered clear of it throughout my middle school years, instead choosing to play volleyball and basketball.

I tried out for the volleyball team my freshman year in high school. Unfortunately I didn't make the team, so I then went to try out for drama a couple weeks later. However, the minute the drama coordinator informed us that we had to sing for tryouts, I was out of there in a heartbeat! Quickly leaving the building before the drama coordinator could stop me, I happened upon the cheerleaders' practice.

For some unknown reason, I sat down and watched them for a while, studying exactly what they had to do. To my amazement, I realized all the stereotypes and rumors about these cheerleaders did not ring true! These cheerleaders were far from being dumb, or whatever else society had made them out to be.

One of my friends was on the freshman squad. So I didn't think it would be too harmful to try out the next time Clinics came along… Before long, tryouts was upon us and I didn't do too hot the first day, but the coach assured me that I could and would do better the next day. The next day rolled around and I was pumped up to prove to the coach that she was right--I could do this. By the end of the day, I knew in my heart, that I would make it.

Still, I did not believe it when the coach told me that I had actually made it. I truthfully thought she was playing a joke on me. But sure enough I had indeed made the team and soon got fitted for my uniform!

I found myself having the time of my life! For once, I was genuinely happy. When the coach finally handed me my fitted uniform, I urged my mother to rush home, so I could get a good look at myself in the mirror. As soon as I put it on, I knew I was hooked for life…

I finally felt like I belonged to something special. I knew that soon everyone at school would know who I was...a cheerleader that could pump up the audience at football games! That, to me, was so incredible and I felt so blessed that my coach had bestowed the honor upon me!

Cheerleading has exposed me to much better life experiences than I had known before. I am grateful to all of my cheer friends who have brought out the best in me. When I first made the team, the other cheer members couldn't understand why a "tough" girl like me wanted to participate in a sport such as cheerleading. I used to be extremely quiet, and prior to cheer, admittedly a bit defensive. Now that I have shown my true colors, my teammates tease me good-naturedly about what a sentimentalist I truly am. I always thought that it was that others "just needed to get to know me" but in reality, all along it was that I simply needed to accept myself. Thank you Cheer! I love you!!!

Justyne Johnson

Magic Pills

Magic is believing in yourself, if you can do that, you can make anything happen. ~Foka Gomez

As I was running errands earlier today, I met a wise old elf. She was very pleasant and asked why I was in such a hurry. I told her I had a cheerleading practice with you girls--our last one before competition.

"Cheerleaders?" she asked. "Are they any good?"

Well, being the proud coach that I am, I responded, "Of course, when they put their minds to it!"

"So tell me more," she asked, and I sat down and told her about each and every one of you. When we were all finished with our chat, she was pleased that I had taken the time to be with her. She was so impressed that she sent along a gift for each of you. She told me that if you followed the directions exactly as they were, you would shine at competition tomorrow…

These are magic "pills" to be taken very specifically and carefully. Look over their descriptions and consider your needs before you do anything:

The BLUE pills are for helping you to stick your stunts (whether you base, spot or fly) and any tumbling passes that you do.

The RED pills are for mighty Team spirit - to help keep it shining through.

The GREEN pills will make your jumps strong and powerful so that you'll seem to be flying.

The ORANGE pills are for mighty voices that will keep strong and not seem to be dying.

The YELLOW pills help to make you smile - you know you're winners with those great grins!!!

The BROWN pills are to help pull it all together - no matter what anybody else says - we all know you're WINNERS!!!

The way these "pills" work is very strange indeed. You may take one each (up to three) for the three things you think you need the most help with, no more than 24 hours (one day) before the event. At the event, you can only take three other "pills" before you perform. Try to save at least one of every color! After you finish your turn, the elf said, if you eat one of every color immediately, your routine will stick in the judges' memories...

The elf also told me to share this "BEWARE" with you. If you take them in any way other than the way she said, the results could be B-A-D!!! She wouldn't say how - but I don't want to see - do you?

Sheila Angalet

NOTE: The "pills" can be any small colorful candy. Remember—it's not the actual "pills" that matter, it's the belief behind them!

For the Dancer

To dance is to be out of yourself, more powerful, more beautiful. This is power, it is glory on earth and it is yours for the taking . ~Agnes De Mille

Feel the music-

Free your soul.

Forget your problems-

Take control.

Spread your wings-

Jump and fly.

Go beyond your limits-

Reach past the sky.

Leap higher than you did before-

Take a risk and dance on a foreign floor.

Make sure you don't lose your focus-

Make sure to always spot;

Don't settle for less than you desire-

Go ahead and take the lot.

Let dedication guide your will-

Have devotion guide your heart;

If on the way intimidation finds you-

Let determination handle that part.

Always keep your chin up-

To all fellow dancers be kind;

Forever point your toes-

And know when not to follow your mind.

Deborah Logozzo

Making the Most of the New Millennium

High achievement always takes place in the framework of high expectation. ~Jack Kinder

In just its third year of existence, 2,000 athletes from 150 schools nationwide are participating in competitive cheerleading. This solidarity has brought cheerleading as a sport to the public eye. To the competitive cheerleader, a state championship is a goal, but when it is achieved it is only one milestone in a world of thousands. On February 14, 1998 I was crowned with seventeen others as state champions. On February 15, I wanted to work harder, to become more...

I realized, however, that if no other goals were to be achieved, I am more. Not only am I an athlete, but I am also wise in that my pursuit has taught me the skills of the survival of the fittest. The discipline required to succeed kept me free from drugs and violence. The expectations I had for myself kept me focused on learning. Perseverance and endurance went hand in hand with school spirit and the internal drive to better myself daily. This commitment forced me to surrender numerous hours each day, working to make peace with my imperfections and to improve. Teamwork taught me to subdue my urge to criticize others.

Every practice I chanted to myself, "Why am I doing this? I won't try out next year." Not to my surprise, I am doing it again this year. My desire to succeed was too strong. I am not a quitter. This commitment and desire to achieve strongly prepares me to live in the 21st century. With the knowledge gained from my experiences, and the quest to continually learn, I will strive to contribute to my environment, Planet Earth.

Danielle Johnson

The Sky is the Limit!

***I believe I can fly. I believe I can touch the sky.** ~**R. Kelly**

Every kid watches "Saved by the Bell", "90210", or some other teenage sitcom that depicts cheerleaders as the greatest. They're pretty, admired, popular, and most importantly, the boys always seem to like them. My whole life I had wanted to possess all of those qualities. I was determined to be a cheerleader.

My name is Kate, and I am an overweight teenager. Being overweight is nothing new to me; I have been overweight for most of my life. Because of my weight, not many boys have really liked me and in the past, I lacked self-esteem. Through most of elementary and junior high, I felt extremely alone and isolated. I felt like people judged me and disregarded any ability I might have, cheer or otherwise.

Going into high school, I was determined to try out and make the cheer squad. I was so scared. There were so many girls there, and they were all so pretty and so very skinny. I was more than scared—I was petrified. Petrified, but still very determined! Having taken dance lessons for ten years, I knew I could do anything they put in front of me. During the week of tryouts, I had also practiced every day for at least five hours a night. I knew the drills inside and out. However, I didn't know if they wanted to see it performed by a 'fat' girl.

The final tryout day arrived. There were fifteen judges on the panel, including four prominent football players. Of course with my luck, I stood smack-dab right in front of them the entire tryout! However, I did my best, and I hoped and prayed that it was good enough to land me a place on the team.

The list was posted the very next day. I went, I saw, and boy did I cry. I could hardly finish reading the list before my eyes filled with tears. I hadn't made the team. There was a crowd of boys hanging out around the list who tormented me. I was so upset; I even made my mom go back to make sure I just didn't miss my name.

As you could probably guess this did nothing to boost my self-esteem. What was I thinking? Who in their right mind would want me, a fat girl, to be a cheerleader? These thoughts dominated my every moment. My already low self-esteem dropped significantly lower. However, somehow, I learned to put the past far enough behind me to try and move on with my life.

The next year I transferred to a new school just in time for cheer tryouts. I was anxious; I didn't want history to repeat itself and I definitely didn't want to have to face that rejection all over again. But, after much consideration, I decided—Hey, what the heck I only live once. Tryouts came and went and I know I did the very best that I could.

Again, the list was posted the next day. I went, I saw, but this time instead of tears of sadness there were tears of joy. I had made the team! For the first time in my life, I felt accepted and special.

A varsity cheerleader, I am now in my third year of my high school cheer career. Even better, I am the team's co-captain. I have also been blessed to receive the "Cheerleader of the Year" award--an award given to a single cheerleader and voted upon by all three levels of cheer.

Who would have ever thought?

Unbeknownst to me, being my last and senior year, my coach and team wanted to do something special for me. It had always been a dream of mine to be a flyer. Due to my size, I knew it could never be a reality, but hey, hadn't I learned that there is nothing wrong with dreaming? Every day after practice, I went home and practiced technique. I did libs and extensions on my sofa couch and I even did cradles on my bed!

One day during practice my coach had three of our boys put me up into an elevator. I was so amazed; I was flying; it was a dream come true! As soon as they had me in the elevator, the next thing I knew I was put in a full extension. I was definitely nervous, but more than anything, I was thrilled!

At our next practice, my coach taught us a new time-out called 'Kate's'. In the center, holding a sign, I went up in a full extension! The first time we did it at a football game I was definitely on cloud nine! Everyone was cheering for ME! The crowd wasn't yelling the usual words; they were yelling and screaming MY name! All the names that people used to call me, all the rejection I had faced, and every bad thing that had ever happened to me just poof!--disappeared. I was undeniably the happiest person alive!

Cheerleading has given me self-esteem, friends, confidence, and most importantly, a second family. My teammates have taught me it doesn't matter what size you are, what you look like, or how many friends you have, all that really matters is the person inside. I am no longer Kate, the fat girl that is too scared to do anything because she's afraid to fail. I am Kate, the girl who does everything to the best of her ability!

I mean, if I can be a flyer, I can do anything. The sky is the limit!!

Kate Lospalluto

Stung

"Defeat may test you; it need not stop you."

It's unbelievable.
The pressure's so thick.
My stomach is churning.
I'm gonna be sick.

My heart is pounding
Like a hammer and a nail.
Because I don't want to
Step out there and fail.

Our coach speaks words
Of encouragement to all.
"Snap it, yell it,
and for God's sake
don't fall!"

The team holds hands
As we say our last prayer.
Before we load our baskets
That fly high in the air.

Our team is announced
To take the floor,
To perform our routine
For the crowd to adore.

The music comes on
As we begin the first dance.

Everything's going fine—
We might even have a chance!

The tumblers are awesome.
Our motions are tight.
Our voices are loud
As we yell, "GO! FIGHT!"

Our coach is ecstatic.
Everything has gone well.
Then what, to my left,
An important stunt fell!

Unbelievable, it's unreal.
This never happened before.
Not once in competition
Have our stunts hit the floor.

The excitement we had
Out on the floor disappeared.
Our big smiles and our glee
Turned to frowns and to tears.

The coach tells us
To still keep our chins raised high.
And never to let anyone
See our high spirit die.

It was a very sad day
For all of us to see
Our hopes and our dreams

Dashed by the sting of a bee!

But that's okay—
Because we still have next year
To prove to the nation
How great we can cheer.

Idris Boyer

With A Smile on My Face

***The mark of a great player is in his ability to come back. The great champions have all come back from defeat.* ~ Sam Snead**

During my freshman year at Ursuline, our brother school Jesuit, had big plans of reviving their drill team. After enduring an extremely tough ordeal, I made the Rangerettes. I had so much fun our charter year, that I decided to take on a bigger role on the team. So I tried out for an officer position for my sophomore season. Unfortunately, I didn't make it.

My sophomore year came and went, and when tryouts rolled around, I again set my sights on making officer. Again, I didn't make it. The year continued, and like the two years prior, the season flew by and tryouts was upon us yet again.

This was it--my last chance at making officer. Seven girls were auditioning altogether; the other six were going into their junior year and I into my last. Being the only senior added to my stress. Leading up to the tryouts I worked especially hard. Besides going to every practice, I stayed at the school nightly, practicing alone in the empty cafeteria. I stretched for hours and did at least a 100 kicks. The tryouts would consist of the execution of splits and kicks, two routines and an interview. By hook or by crook, I planned on acing every part.

Finally the big day came. Out of the seven candidates, I was the last to tryout. For the next hour and a half in wait, I did nothing but psych myself.

My moment arrived. I took my position before the panel of four judges and the music started. I did my routine perfectly--hitting every leap, and executing every split perfectly. Flashing a final smile at the panel of judges, I saw one return mine with a huge one of her own.

During my interview the panel drilled me with questions. Using my three years of experience, I answered the questions confidently. Again, I left with a smile on my face.

After my interview, I anxiously waited in the hallway with my six other teammates. After what seemed like an eternity, but in reality was only five minutes, we were beckoned. Following tradition, we each took our place in a line, sat down and looked directly ahead. We longingly glanced at the table in front of us where five bears dressed in officer attire sat. An elected officer would soon have one of the treasured bears placed in front of her.

We all closed our eyes. After what seemed like hours, the retired officers asked everyone to open them. I couldn't. I was so scared. With my eyes closed, I felt Ellen, the girl sitting next to me, hug me. Right then I knew it. I hadn't made it.

It was the hardest moment of my life--sitting there and realizing after three years and three tryouts, I hadn't made it. Climbing into my car I cried and cried. For the thirty-minute drive home, my sorrow was my only companion.

Two hours later my mother got home. With a smile in her voice, she called out to me. She didn't know; she just assumed that I had made it. I ran from my room and into her arms and cried and cried some more.

"Oh baby, oh my darling," she cried and I buried my head into her shoulder. Soon, I realized that I wasn't the only one crying. We stayed like that for a good five minutes, weeping together for my wretched situation.

Six months later, I am now about to finish my first semester of my senior year. I want to tell everyone, it's okay. I'm okay. Disappointment plays a part in any activity, but the important thing to remember is to always hold your head high. You'll make it through it, just like I did, and you're bound to come out a stronger person.

My dad had wanted me to quit drill team right then and there, but I couldn't and didn't. I stayed with it. Those who have everything given to them can really never appreciate the finer things of life. Those of us who have to work for it, come out with a greater understanding of how precious life can be. And perhaps, like me, they can continue on with smiles on their faces.

Karin Burk

Whirlwind of Courage

Courage permits the caliber of performance to continue at its peak, until the finish line is crossed. ~Stuart Walker

The whirlwind of courage,

that creeps up to my spirit,

looks me in the eyes,

and begs me to hear it.

I listen to it carefully,

I listen to it all.

It tells me to lift up my chin,

to stand proud and tall.

It says to keep my spirit,

running loud and high,

to listen to my strength,

and with that I did reply,

"I will keep this promise

and I will hold it dear

because I know with strength and courage,

victory is near."

Rachel Carpenter

spirit

When there is nothing else, there's spirit."

Got Spirit?

"I guess you can say that I am a spirit leader. That's why God made me a cheerleader."

There's an immeasurable feeling inside me that burns just like a flame.

This feeling gets me pumped up before, during and after every game.

When I get this feeling I jump, smile and shout.

There is just no denying it—this feeling is Spirit, without a doubt.

Spirit makes me feel as if I'm on the top--

Once I get the Spirit I truly can't be stopped.

Spirit runs through my body like the blood in my veins.

Without the Spirit, I'm really not the same.

Whether my team wins or loses my Spirit remains high.

Without Spirit my team would never ever get by.

Spirit is as good for me as calcium and juice.

Once I taste the good stuff I simply cut loose.

I guess you can say that I'm a Spirit leader.

That's why God made me a cheerleader.

Cheerleading is that Something that I love to do.

So I say, "I've got the Spirit!

How about you?"

Christi Lee

Ready to Face the World

It's not whether you get knocked down, it's whether you get up.
~Vince Lombardi

Being an NCA instructor, I am blessed with many opportunities to visit different places and interact with scores of people. During the summer of 1998, I felt especially fortunate to cross paths with an exceptionally amazing young lady.

It was my second summer as an instructor and I had been appointed as the buddy instructor for several cheerleaders. We had just finished reviewing the morning's material and were heading off to lunch, when a girl from my buddy squad walked over to me. Now, this was a gal who was always smiling and always ready and willing to try anything. Her whole attitude reflected everything positive about cheerleading. I couldn't help but smile as she bounced over to me. Grinning from ear-to-ear, I asked her if she was having fun.

"Yeah! But I'm not going to be here this afternoon or tonight. My mom's coming to pick me up, but I'll be back tomorrow," she answered.

"Okay, great," I said, "I'll see you tomorrow!"

I watched her as she ran off to join her teammates. I hadn't asked her why she would be gone for the rest of the afternoon and hadn't given it much thought until I met with her team later in the day. While the team was warming up, I noticed her absence and asked one of her teammates why she had left camp for the day.

Her teammate informed me that the girl's father had been sick for a long time and that he had passed away that very morning. I told the teammate that the girl didn't have to come back the next day and that she should take the time to be with her family. Her teammate assured me though, that the girl had been so excited and happy about going to camp, that she would definitely be back the next day.

My heart just about shattered to know that the young girl, who couldn't have been more than fourteen, was planning to come back to camp after just losing her father. What was left of my broken heart melted later on in the day, when I talked to the girl's coach about the situation. The coach explained to me that it was cheerleading that was getting this brave girl through the difficult time with her father's sickness. This was the first time the girl had been to camp and she simply didn't want to miss anything.

I have to admit that I wasn't expecting her to show up the next day, given the circumstances. However, as I walked over to my buddy group the following morning, I saw her sitting there amongst her teammates. There she was…with a smile on her face… ready to face the day.

Later, as I watched her graduate from her first NCA camp, I realized that her return was her way of proving that she was ready to face the world!

To that little girl, who left a mark on my heart, I'd like to say thank you for the blessing that you are!

Brittany Geragotelis

Soul Mates

Two souls with but a single thought, two hearts that beat as one.
~Frederick Halm

As the co-owner of a company that operates children's dance programs in over one hundred communities, I had the challenging job of finding the right individual to work in our office and help coordinate all one hundred directors.

The right individual needed to be very special as she would need to wear so many hats. She would handle parent phone calls, motivate the instructors, lead training workshops, teach dances and institute new policies. In essence she would be an extension of myself. I strongly felt that this person needed to have a good value system and be able to deal with issues the way I would personally deal with them. She would need to be intelligent, have a charismatic personality and be self-motivated.

I searched through my mind for people I had worked with in the past or had made contact with through our summer camps. Each year I work with thousands of dancers, coaches, and instructors. I mulled over my many options and kept coming back to Carrie Kavanaugh.

Carrie had been my dance assistant while she attended the community college. She had long since left our small town and had gone on for her four-year degree. Years had passed and she now worked in downtown Minneapolis for a consulting firm. I didn't really think she would even be interested but I thought it wouldn't hurt to contact her.

I didn't have her current phone number so I called her parents. Luckily, they still had the same number and her mom answered the phone. I explained to her who I was and told her that I was trying to reach her daughter. She gave me her present number.

Unbeknownst to me, when Carrie's mom rung off with me, she promptly called Carrie at work…

"Cindy Clough returned your call," she informed Carrie.

Dumb-founded, Carrie sat in silence momentarily. "But Mom…I haven't called her yet!" she replied.

Apparently, for quite some time, Carrie had felt that she needed to make some changes in her life. She had come to the realization that the career she had chosen and had studied tediously for in college was not quite what she wanted. After some soul-searching she had mentioned to her mom that she would love to move back to Brainerd to work full-time for my company, Just For Kix.

Within three weeks of my initial call, Carrie was working in the Just For Kix corporate offices.   In that short span of time, she had quit her job, moved back to Brainerd, and found her way back into my life.

Carrie and I always wonder what drew us back together. Was it fate, coincidence or divine intervention? Whatever it was, it was obviously meant to be. We hadn't talked for years and then out of the blue we both felt and filled a big "need" for the other person!

Whatever it was...we're just glad it happened.

Cindy Clough

Getting Involved

Enlightenment must come little by little… ~Idries Shah

School spirit had never really been my strong suit. My best friend had been a cheerleader most of her life and I was never really interested in it. However, at the end of my sophomore year she talked me into trying out for the mascot position. I acted as if it were of no consequence but I was ecstatic when I made it.

I learned so much that first year. I had never previously realized how involved a cheerleader had to be. It wasn't just about pep rallies and the football games. We performed at basketball games, parades, charity events, and even kindergarten pep rallies. Cheerleading filled an empty space and took up the extra time I had on my hands. It made high school so much more exciting.

Now I am a senior and I'm more involved than ever. I am still the mascot and I plan on trying out for the college position as well. Cheerleading has enlightened me to a whole new meaning of "school spirit." I hope my best friend realizes how much she helped change my life!

Debra Olds

True Champions

Character is what you know you are, not what others think you have.
~Marva Collins.

My squad had just finished their routine and it was a bit shaky. We thought we might win third place in the co-ed division, but when the awards were handed out, Mariner High School placed third.   My team accepted the results and seemed to take the news well.

About fifteen minutes later, as I was packing up my cheer bag, Mary Beth Crowder, the coach from Mariner High School informed me that she had found a mistake in the scoring and had reported it to the organizers of the competition. It turned out that Oak Harbor had actually scored 7 points higher than Mariner and that we had actually placed 3rd. She told me that the organizers were going to send a trophy to us in the mail and that Mariner could keep the third-place trophy.   I was very impressed with Mariner's coach's integrity.

Just after I finished telling my squad the news, the coach of the Mariner team tapped me on the shoulder and with her entire team standing beside her, said, " My cheerleaders want your cheerleaders to have this trophy. They feel that Oak Harbor rightfully deserves the trophy, not them and they insist that you have it!"

I was overwhelmed to tears. I encouraged them to keep it but they wouldn't; they truly wanted Oak Harbor to have the trophy.

Competition day is always filled with excitement, anticipation, happiness, sadness, disappointment and triumph but that day my cheerleaders and I learned the true essence of "champion". The "true champions" were Mariner High School Cheerleaders and their coach, Mary Beth Crowder. They may not have won first place; but for years to come, my team will always remember Mariner High School Cheerleaders for their character and sportsmanship. What a wonderful life lesson of integrity and sportsmanship these young adults had taught us!

My squad had a trophy made for Mariner High school with the inscription "NW Cheerleading Championship 1st Place Sportsmanship Award". I wrote a letter to their principal and athletic director informing them what outstanding representatives their cheerleaders were for Mariner High School. They personified the true meaning of cheerleading.

Pam Headridge

Lifelong Friendship

From Spirited Rivals to Kindred Spirits, Cheerleaders Build a Lifelong Friendship

The NCA Large Junior High/Middle School National Championship Title was a tough one to take from Carl Albert Junior High.   Of Midwest City, Oklahoma, the cheerleaders had clinched the title the past 6 out of 8 years. Last year's .06 loss, however, by Martin Middle School of Martin, Tennessee to First Place Champion Carl Albert set the stage for some fierce competition.   But it was also the beginning of something much bigger, a bond that far exceeded winning any championship title.

When a tornado tore through the city of Midwest, Oklahoma on May 3, of 1999 it also tore through the hearts of the Martin Middle School cheerleading team.   Their biggest competitors at Carl Albert were in need of some help. With compassion, they set their intense rivalry aside as the team gathered gifts and wrote personal messages of support to every girl on the squad. That loving gesture was enough to turn around the power of the sometimes cutthroat and emotional battle that imbues the cheerleading industry.

Returning this time to the Dallas Convention Center for the 18th Annual NCA High School Championship, the tears were of a different sort. Just minutes after losing to Martin Middle School by 25/100th of a point in the Tuesday prelims, the Carl Albert squad met up with their competitors to strengthen their union and share their gratitude. Carl Albert cheerleaders gave the Martin Middle School squad t-shirts that read "Cheer Competitor-Life Friends."   Between the prose, two girls in their school colors holding hands, one with pigtails resembling Martin's competitive hairstyle and the other with a ponytail, the Carl Albert look.

In the end, their hearts united, their titles defined. Martin Middle School went on to take First Place with a 9.07 edging out Carl Albert with a 8.56. It was a dream come true for the Martin cheerleading team and its coach who had worked incredibly hard to overcome last year's defeat.

However, as is any lesson in life, the meaning here goes far beyond the championship title. For both teams, the kindness of humanity put competition in its place. They learned that in the end, it does not matter whether you win or lose, it's the spirit in your heart that counts and the spirit in your heart that wins. Thus, giving meaning to the *Spirit of Competition*!

Susan Havens

Athletes are...

Is there a limit? Athletes don't think that way. ~Bill Rogers

What makes an athlete is something rare.

It's not size or the color of skin or hair.

It's not whom you know or where you have been.

It's how hard you work and how much time you spend.

It's inner spirit and determination

That makes an athlete an inspiration.

The little kids, yeah, they look and act upon

What we do with and without that uniform on.

We're cheerleaders, dancers and coaches too.

We know that we're athletes...

What about you?

Lauren Muckleroy

The True Cheerleader

The question is not whether we will die, but how we will live. ~Joan Borysenko

Having been an NFL Cheerleader for the past five seasons, I have often been asked what my crowning moment as a professional cheerleader is. When being questioned I am usually on the defensive, trying to convince those that my job is indeed professional and very worthwhile. I'll often refer to the 1997 Pro Bowl where I represented and cheered for the St. Louis Rams. Other times, I am as apt to refer to the impressive USO Tour to Japan.

In professional athletics the opportunity to travel, meet influential people, and rub shoulders with the greatest competitors in the world is certainly enticing. I have always viewed this opportunity as the result of my hard work and ambition. I am proud of what I have accomplished and know that I have earned all that I have achieved. Last year I was especially blessed with the opportunity to briefly encounter someone who changed my life, my perceptions and my future.

One morning a mother entered my classroom in tears. She told me a woeful tale of a sick child who, coincidentally, wanted very much to meet some Rams Cheerleaders. Having overheard this sad conversation, my students began buzzing amongst themselves. They began to create a 'Get Well' banner for the boy. They pulled things from their desks, from the shelves, and out of my file cabinets. Pencils, stickers, folders, games and anything else they thought the boy might like were assembled into a basket. To my amazement, the children had set up shop right in the middle of my classroom floor.

Before I knew it, the lunch bell had rung and we had not accomplished one academic thing all morning. Michael, my prized art student, a bit disinterested in school at the time, grabbed Bradley and began to draw a huge Tasmanian Devil in the middle of the banner.

"All kids like Taz! This will make him feel better," Michael told me, without missing a stroke. The children, one by one, carefully wrote warm wishes on the banner. They handled the banner as if it were made from exclusive silk.

At the end of the day the students and I were exhausted. We had not solved one math problem, answered one essay question, nor proved any scientific theorems.

However, I felt that I had learned more in that one day from my students than I could have ever imagined possible. To top it off, the next day my students had brought so many coloring books and Beanie Babies from home that we had to get a bigger basket! Someone had also been thoughtful and ingenious enough to add a Rams baseball cap to the collection!

The big day finally arrived. My friend and fellow cohort, Amy joined me to meet the boy at a promotion for The Children's Miracle Network. I'll never forget the way I felt awaiting the child's arrival. Every time a child walked through the door I prayed that it wouldn't be him. I couldn't imagine what I could possibly say to him or his family.

As I reached down to grab my pom pons from my bag, I heard a cheerful little giggle coming my way. Looking up, I caught sight of the little boy that would change my life forever. Before my eyes appeared the most precious little face belonging to the most beautiful little boy I had ever seen. His deep blue eyes pierced straight through to my heart. His name was Sean.

After the proper introductions, Sean rifled through his basket. His eyes widened at the life-like Taz that popped out of the banner. He looked up at me, grinned, and informed me that Taz was indeed his favorite cartoon character. Before I knew what had hit me, I had set up shop in the middle of the floor just like my students had! I was completely oblivious to the other shoppers and my surroundings.

In my lap, with his Ram's cap worn backwards, he told me of his great adventures. He told me how he had met the St. Louis Blues hockey players and "Big Mak" of the St. Louis Cardinals, and how he loved Bob Costas because he had a "neat" new wing at the hospital. While playing patty cake, we chatted about Mickey Mouse and his trip to Disney.

He saved his greatest adventure, however, for last. Hopping out of my lap, he turned so that he could get a good look at my reactions as he told his favorite story.

"I am an Honorary Fireman," he said as he shook his head and puckered his lips to emphasize just how unbelievably cool he was.

"Stop it, " I said, in amazement, as if I could not believe my ears. He picked up my hand firmly to convince me that he was completely telling the truth. He described the ceremony and explained how his uniform was NOT a costume but an authentic. He absolutely loved the firemen, their trucks, and their uniforms. Somehow I just knew that Sean had captured their spirit just as he had captured mine.

As Sean played, his mother and I took the time to talk. I was amazed at her ability to comfort me, a complete stranger. Although I could sense her fatigue, I couldn't help but feel her integrity and the everlasting spirit that she had so successfully instilled in her son. Sean was just like her!

We said our good-byes and promised to keep in touch. As Sean walked out the door I asked him what his plans for the rest of the day were. Sean turned, flashing his darling little dimples, and said, "Play with all my new stuff, Silly."

That was the last time I would ever see Sean.

The next day at school my students couldn't wait to hear all about him. Michael and Bradley beamed as I told them how much Sean loved the banner. Michael put his head down on his desk, perhaps finally realizing that HE too was somebody really special. I passed a picture of Sean around the room as we talked about how that dear little boy had captivated my attention.

"It was as if he were the cheerleader," I told my students. This perfect little spirited soul was cheering for life and everything life had to offer. He didn't act sick. He didn't seem scared. Sean was cheering the celebration of life!

One afternoon I came home to the message that Sean had died. I felt so terribly guilty that I had not been able to say good-bye. That afternoon was a tough one at school. We passed Sean's picture around the room, used a lot of tissue, and stapled Sean's pictures upon the bulletin board. I think perhaps Michael took the news the hardest.

My mother accompanied me on the trip to the funeral home because I didn't want to drive alone. Lost on our way, and just about ready to give up, we were startled by a loud sound. My mother pointed out the window and instantly I knew we were at the right place. The sound had come from a monstrous, red fire truck that was flying a flag over the funeral home…a tribute to one of their own men.

All of Sean's special "stuff" was on display, revealing the story of his great adventures. His Beanie Babies, autographed jerseys, and pictures were all reminders of the joy he had brought to everything and everyone he touched. I tried not to look at the pictures as I stood in line, for I didn't think I could keep myself together. However, I caught a glimpse of the picture of Sean and two Rams Cheerleaders.

As I approached the casket, begging God to help me, I looked straight into the devastated eyes of the fireman standing guard at Sean's side. He stood statuesque, with chin quivering and tears streaming down his face. Everyone shared his grief. I touched the closed casket and thanked Sean for sharing his spirit and love of life. I promised him that from that day on that I would live everyday with his dear spirited soul.

I am teaching the fifth grade now. I keep Sean's pictures in one of my most treasured books. One day during silent reading, one of my students found his picture and asked me who he was. It was time to share Sean's gift of spirit and soul. He will live inside of me forever.

Now ask me please what my greatest moment as a Rams cheerleader is. I will tell you about an encounter with someone who taught me the true meaning of life, love, and the gift of the human spirit. A true cheerleader, a lover of life! My fondest memory comes back to me each time I see a shiny fire truck blazing down the street. I think of Sean, with backward cap and all, sounding the siren and calling the shots.

Melissa Pennell-Kimble

'Twas the Night Before the Competition

"It's not what's in our heads, but what's in our hearts that makes us winners."

'Twas the night before the competition,

And we awaited the competitors with anticipation.

The floor was all cleared; the bleachers set in place,

No one yet in the audience, not one single face...

When at the front door we heard a soft chatter,

We thought to ourselves, "What could be the matter?"

And there in the lobby stood thirteen girls,

Decked in shiny gold and black, with their ponytails curled.

Not cheerleaders I thought--too quiet and meek.

But they proved me wrong, the next day at the meet.

They cheered with spirit and their moves were ever so tight,

I forgot what I was doing and watched them--

They were simply out of sight!

Their cheers on the floor were ever so clean,

Only to be bettered by their great stunt routine.

Their eyes had a sparkle when they looked in my direction

Their cheer for their team was done to almost perfection.

One round left to cover, could all that practice be for naught?

But they jumped with such height with not a second thought.

We all wondered in amazement, what gave them the stuff

To make them so great, and ever so tough?

Was it their coach, their parents, or just something they did?

That made us all wish that this team was "our kids."

The trophies were stacked from their necks to their knees,

When we asked them their secret they smiled with ease.

"It's not our coach or our parents that force us to be good.

But they've taught us the basics and the things that they should.

It's not what's in our heads, but what's in our hearts

That makes us winners, and sets us apart."

As they walked out the door with their bags held tight,

They looked over their shoulders and whispered,

"Congratulations to all and to all a Good Night!"

Ali Ropes

So What?

For a righteous man falls seven times, and rises again.
~Proverbs 24:16

I have many memories from my years as a cheerleader. Having been the captain my senior year, you'd think that my most memorable moment would come from that particular season. It's not. Instead, the memory that first comes to mind comes from my junior year when I was not a captain, but a base.

Our squad had intensely practiced a halftime cheer for an upcoming game against one of our rivals. Time and time again, we hit everything perfectly in practice.

The night of the big game came and we were pumped. We hit smoothly, until we attempted our stunt line at the end of the routine. I dropped the flyer. Stunned beyond belief, I mechanically picked her up off the ground.

The squad walked off the floor with forced smiles. We were embarrassed to the point that we all wanted to quit.

However, the flyer I dropped said, "So what? We made a mistake. No one was hurt and we walked off with smiles on our faces. I say we did very well."

With that, we were again ready to dominate the sidelines. When the game resumed, we cheered our hearts out.

Darla S. Bandt

A Family Tradition

"Somewhere in the stands is a little girl who want to be just like you."

Homecoming 1989. On this warm September Saturday afternoon, Standley Lake High School's football stadium was packed with hundred of fans. Blue, green, and white balloons swayed cheerfully in the wind; the crowd sang a boisterous fight song and the cheerleaders fervently cheered for their winning team. All were proud to be Gators.   For the first time in the high school's very short history, the football team had played and won their homecoming game.

In the midst of it all sat a little girl. Sitting in the bleachers, she watched the cheerleaders with rapt concentration. Her eyes often lingered on one particular cheerleader, her big sister Kelly. Being only seven years old, she would treasure this first memory of high school. Later that night the little girl again engrossingly watched her sister prepare for the first annual Homecoming dance. All decked out and ready to dance the night away, the older sister looked stunning as she left for the dance.

Homecoming 1990.   The bleachers again were filled with Gator fans. Despite the Gators 27-50 loss to the Wheatridge Farmers, many Gator fans were still looking forward to the evening's Homecoming Dance. Amidst the excitement and the decorations, a little girl, standing behind the fence, focused on the cheerleaders. She now closely observed two of the cheerleaders, her two older sisters Kelly and Erica. That evening, the little girl watched her two sisters adorn themselves for the night ahead. With their hair swept up, their make-up expertly applied, and their beautiful dresses worn, the two older sisters made quite a spectacle as they left for the Homecoming Dance with their dates.

Homecoming 1991. A success. Enthusiastic and spirited, students crammed the stadium that night in order to see the Gators sweep Evergreen. Holding her green pom pons, the same little girl cheered on the Gators. The following Saturday afternoon, the little girl joyously beheld her two big sisters get ready for another big Homecoming dance. As always, they looked beautiful.

Painted faces could be seen from everywhere, and voices of Gator fans could be heard from a mile away. Like the previous three years, the 1994 Homecoming game was a huge success.   As the Gators defeated the Arvada West Wildcats, students jumped to their feet cheering on the football team. The stands were filled with fans and decorations, and in the midst, the same little girl watched the cheerleaders. However, she no longer watched Kelly or Erica. She now kept a close eye on her third older sister, Angela. The following night, the little girl watched Angela dress for the big dance. Angela looked beautiful. As Angela headed out of the house in her beautiful black dress, the little girl just knew Angela and her date were ready to dance the night away.

The following two years, this little girl religiously attended the Homecoming games to watch her sister cheer on the Gators. Like usual, fans filled the bleachers to the brim, overflowing with spirit and enthusiasm. From the bleachers, the little girl smiled at her sister Angela as she started yet another cheer. Again, and yet again, she watched her sister get all dressed up and all decked out for the Homecoming dance. And like always, Angela was a knock-out.

Homecoming 1999. Being the football program's 10th year anniversary, school spirit was at an all-time high. Decorated cars, painted faces, and waving flags could be seen everywhere—all in support of the wondrous Gators. As the fourth quarter ended, the crowd ran onto the field to celebrate. The football team took off their helmets, and all at once, about 300 students sang the traditional fight song. The Homecoming game was the biggest success ever. The Gator football team had defeated their Pomona rivals for the first time in Standley Lake history. Exhilaration surged through the stadium. The cheerleaders led the exuberant fans in spirit.

But this year, something was different about the Homecoming game. The little girl could no longer be found in the stands. She, in fact, was now a cheerleader. Her sisters were now watching her perform from the bleachers. She had already cheered for three exciting Homecoming games and had attended all the dances.

I was that little girl. I am now sixteen and my dream of cheering for Standley Lake has finally come true. Whether my older sisters realize it or not, this all could not have taken place had they not inspired me. Kelly, Erica, and Angela have always been, and will always be, my greatest sources of inspiration. "Once a Gator, always a Gator!"

Lyndsey Kilpatrick

The Champion

Confidence, that is everything. ~Ilie Natase

"Why would she give you her collegiate national championship ring?" asked the amazed teenager.

She and I had been discussing her dance team and the thrill of competition. I had shared with her my daughter Courtney's own experiences of competition—how high standards, technique, teamwork and dedication had made their national undertaking a success. When I showed her Courtney's ring she was incredulous that my daughter would have even taken it off her finger.

"For years, Courtney watched and danced along as I coached the high school dance team," I explained.

Realizing that at the age of seven, Courtney was capable of more than what my team was currently doing, I set out to find a good ballet class to enroll her in. In doing so, I, at the age of thirty-one, began taking classes again. Despite our age difference, we shared a common love of music and dance. As time went on our love and her ability simultaneously grew...

"When she got to high school, she became a cheerleader. She had the time of her life," I continued.

Whether on the football field or on the basketball court, she emanated self-confidence every time she cheered. She was vivacious. Courtney loved the camaraderie. She lived for the hype and the excitement of the crowd. But her true love was not cheering on the sidelines; it was dancing on the field.

"So how'd she end up with a national dance championship ring instead of a cheer one?" the enthralled teen asked.

After much discussion, Courtney persuaded me into coaching her cheer team. Understandably, I was very apprehensive. The personality conflicts, strenuous practices and tryouts could lead to numerous problems for her, her friends and me. More importantly, what would it do to our strong mother-daughter relationship?

However, our new arrangement strengthened our feelings of respect for one another and deepened our common love for dance. Coaching her practices, performances, training and workout sessions provided me with a greater understanding of my daughter and what made her tick. Basking in the rays of her self-assurance, determination and strength I found the determination to do with my life what I really wanted to do.

With college in her near future, I encouraged her to try out for the Barton County's dance team, the Cougar Kittens. Sure she had had a great cheer career, but it was obvious that dance was her passion. And what team could possibly be a better team to dance for than one that consistently finished in the top five in its division at Nationals?

Courtney went on and danced with the BCCC dance team. And not to my surprise, they won Nationals. After earning the ring, Courtney sent it with a letter to me...

"It read, 'Without your inspiration and confidence in me, I would not have had the courage to try for my dream. You are my champion and deserve this ring,'" I told the inspired dancer.

The best gift of all was not the ring itself; but what the gift symbolized--the relationship with my daughter. We shared, and continue to share, our joys, disappointments and our victories. Courtney attributes her success to me; the feeling is indeed reciprocated. She and her success give me the inspiration to reach for my dreams.

Jeanette Price

Refreshing Innocence

Innocence is like polished armor; it adorns and defends.
~Bishop Robert South

I coach a team of girls age six to nine who compete at regional and national competitions. Last spring, attending a competition in Dallas, was on our agenda. For the big contest, the girls were to wear the fifties "get-up"—complete with poodle skirts and hair pieces tied up and curled for the definitive ponytail.

En route to Dallas, a cute little blonde named Ashley approached me and said, "Jamie, I feel like we are telling lies."

Confused, I replied, "Why Ashley?"

"Well," she said, "we are acting like we have long hair when actually, we don't!"

I smiled. "Do you ever dress up for Halloween?"

"Yes," she said, nodding her head vigorously.

"Well, putting on the hairpieces is just like wearing a mask or a wig for Halloween. It's just a part of a costume," I explained.

Ashley smiled happily and breathed an audible sigh of relief.

"Good," she said, " because my momma taught me never to lie."

Ahh…refreshing innocence.

Jamie Bond

Last Game

"Cheer each game as if it were your last."

Every year, on a cold night in November, we play our last varsity football game of the season. Every year, without fail, the senior girls on our squad get really emotional and teary-eyed watching the quarters of their last football game fly by.

For the past three years, my friends and I hadn't understood this phenomenon. Amongst ourselves, we always wondered what the big deal was. After all, they were only football games. There would always be more games, year after year after year.

Well, this year was different. This time around, my friends and I were finally the seniors on the squad. When the last game rolled around, we finally realized what the big hubbub had always been about. Feelings overwhelmed us as we stood next to the fence.

Here we were, doing the same thing that we have done over and over again throughout the years. As I cheered there with my squad, watching the final seconds of our last football game, I understood that this was it. Just like that!

Yes, there were going to be many more football games over the years but it wouldn't be the same. We wouldn't be cheering on "our guys" to all the great victories and upsetting defeats. Fighting with the schools' archrivals, cheering at the wild bonfires, and of course, leading the crazy pep rallies would no longer be our privilege.

Right then I realized to have a great time is to always live, laugh, and love what you're doing. The memories that we create and share together will last us a lifetime. These are the days we'll remember...

Shannon Daley

Good-bye

"Never say goodbye, say farewell."

It is time to say good-bye.

Time to let it all go.

I can't believe we

Came so far;

I can't believe four years

Are gone.

It seems like only yesterday

I put on my uniform

For the very first time.

When, in fact,

It was only yesterday

That I put on my uniform

For the very last time.

It's hard to believe how

Much we've grown—

From home-made hippie outfits

To bold and shiny lycra;

From the crowded and noisy hallways

To a silently awestruck audience;

From twenty unacquainted girls

To a strong and unified squad.

And as I look back

And reflect upon these years

I ask myself,

Where did it all go?

How could the weeks

And months of each year

Pass so quickly,

When two hours of practice

Could seem like an eternity?

I've always been

Able to look ahead-

To plan for the future,

To set time

To reach my goals,

To say,

"We'll do it next year."

But time kept slipping

Forward,

And my place here

Kept slipping

Away.

Now I can only wonder

What might have changed.

What should have happened,

What could've been...

If something,

Somebody,

Or I had been different.

And I can be proud of

Our growth,

Proud of every achievement,

Proud of the places we've been,

Proud of everything that is

Yet to be...

And will be done.

And for now

I turn in my uniform

And its accessories:

Two lycra costumes

One shell

A warm-up outfit

Two white gloves

A set of poms

An identity

Some pride

My love

My spirit

And

My place...

To be handed down

And to be carried on...

Melissa Reh

coach

Leadership is action, not a position."

Called To Greatness

Positive thinking creates a positive mind, which then creates positive people. ~Matt Day

Today you are called to greatness

Because cheerleaders call you Coach.

Will you shrink or rise to the occasion?

Will you use the positive approach?

Today you are called to greatness.

Step out of the shadow now.

Don't worry about your shortcomings.

Your heart will show you how.

Your mission is to touch the hearts.

Your goal is to build their skill.

Hold on to the higher vision.

Never worry: you can; you will.

There are many who will need you

As you face your challenging days.

They always demand and drain you;

They will steal your resolve away.

But as a coach you must believe

They can achieve their highest potential.

Just be patient and intent on love

And the growing will be sequential.

Today you are called to greatness

Expectations are set very high.

Can you accept your limitations?

Can you learn and can you try?

Even though the journey seems tough

And you only have so much to give,

Keep belief foremost in your heart

For you teach them how to live.

Today you are called to greatness.

Today your influence goes far.

As a coach you make a difference

You touch them by who you are.

Linda Rae Chappell

Dear Coach

I can only show you the way. It's up to you to go there. ~Larry Ellis

Dear Coach:

From cheerleading to soccer,

Even football it seems,

There is always a source of strength

That supports all the teams…

A woman or man,

A teacher or friend,

A model, an idol

A coach 'til the end…

Whether first or tenth place,

They're the glue on the floor.

Pushing their team towards victory

Striving for more…

There is always that person

That can light up an athlete's face.

And it's you Coach, I know

I can never replace!

Angela Tancredi

Saving Grace

***You may have to fight a battle more than once to win it.* ~Margaret Thatcher**

Everyone has them. Those incredibly brief moments of crystal clarity that reveal amazing insight into the psyche. For me these revelations have shown time and time again that cheerleading is my saving grace.

Looking back at my childhood, it seems quite unremarkable. With the exception of our many moves from house to house, from city to city, that is. My father's job in the aerospace industry required frequent relocation. By the time I had reached sixth grade, I had lived in twelve different houses, in seven cities, in six states. Although I always made friends quickly, I was more often than not, the outsider, the new kid in school. I was emotionally insecure about my value as a person.

Puberty roared fast and furiously into my life. I rapidly transformed from the skinny pixie-like child to a curvaceous young woman. Being one of the first to hit adolescence, I was the butt of many embarrassing jokes and remarks. Always being the outsider, I didn't have any close friend to confide in. Food became my crutch and best friend. I rapidly gained weight.

In the early 70's, 'do your own thing' was the motto of the times. But doing your own thing was only truly acceptable if it encompassed being a carbon copy Twiggy with bone-straight hair! That certainly did not describe me. Being a size thirteen, I felt ostracized by my classmates and society.

I constantly observed the cheerleaders around school. They were all pretty, popular, and well-adored by the boys. They dressed fabulously, looked beautiful and were full of self-confidence. They were always chosen, by teachers and fellow students, for privilege after privilege. Like any other normal girl, I so wanted that life for myself.

But that didn't seem possible. There wasn't any way to look fashionable; the hip clothes weren't made in a size thirteen! My naturally curly hair clashed with the straight look. Although on the surface I may have seemed a happy and well-adjusted person, a great chasm existed in my soul. I was convinced that becoming a cheerleader would bridge it.

I jumped at the first opportunity to try out for the cheerleading squad. Although I never truly believed that I had a chance, I worked hard all week. After the rigorous tryouts, I nervously waited with breathless anticipation for the results. When I discovered that I had actually made the squad, I was dumbfounded. I had never believed that I could become one of the chosen few.

I cheered for a year and that year was like a dream come true. I finally felt connected to the world around me. I felt accepted by my peers. I blossomed. Being a cheerleader boosted my self-confidence. The uniform seemed to be a personality enhancer and boy, did I enjoy it!

I decided not to cheer my last two years in high school. But those two years were just as wonderful as my one year as a cheerleader. Cheerleading had truly improved my life and I lived the after-effects for a long time to come. Now I know that the uniform isn't a magical spell that can miraculously change your life. But the courage, confidence, and strength that were by-products of wearing the uniform made it seem that way.

Years later, in my late-thirties, I found myself unmarried, without kids, and once again, overweight. I felt useless and unnecessary. My life had certainly not turned out the way I had envisioned it would. I relived the severe angst of my teen pre-cheer years. There were days where getting out of bed presented a difficulty. I was simply overwhelmed.

And then cheerleading made its way back into my life...

An elementary school squad, in its first year, had had some serious problems with parents. The coach opted not to return for the second season. Without a coach, the team would cease to exist. I was asked to fill in. Little did anyone know how much this new position would mean to me...

I developed a connection to the cheerleaders and to their parents. I took great joy in developing the young people's values and ideals. I felt needed and useful. Getting up in the morning became easy. I had something to look forward to at the end of the day. My dedication to these hard-working and talented people became a lifeline I treasure to this very day.

Does the politics of cheerleading frustrate me? You bet'cha! However, the joys of coaching and the close friendships I have forged are worth it! My cheerleaders are family to me. And family is too precious to ever let go.

Barbara Overton

Drill Team Mom

A wise parent humors the desire for independent action, so as to become the friend and advisor when his absolute rule shall cease. ~Elizabeth Gaskell

Having been a drill team director for seventeen years, I thought I had handled just about everything at one time or another. But when Heather, my fourteen-year old daughter, decided to try out for the high school drill team, I was thrilled. When she made the team, I was ecstatic. Of course, being in the business for so long, Heather and I knew all the judges; but they had assured me that this had had no bearing on their decision. She simply had had the talent. At last, my "dream" had come true. The passion that I have for drill team had rubbed off on my offspring. Or had it?

Suddenly I have found myself immersed in a new role. With it comes questions that I had not foreseen. Must I be the "normal" mom who watches the nightly living room rehearsals with loving eyes and who lets someone else do the perfecting? Or should I do my job and constantly evaluate and critique? Should I constantly praise, critically analyze or should I just encourage?

When Heather had been in 4th or 5th grade she had been assigned a paper for English. It had been getting late into the evening and she had not completed it by the time she was to go to bed. So she could get a good night's sleep, I finished the paper for her. In it I had used the word 'mere.' After having Heather read the paper aloud in front of the class, the teacher then asked her to define 'mere.' Consequently, I never wrote another paper for my daughter again. Her embarrassment over the incident was, and continues to be, a reminder that a parent can help too much. So with that incident in mind, I have been, and still am, wary about what my actions regarding her dancing career should be.

Due to illness, Heather was unable to attend the first afternoon practices with the team this past week. Today one of the new officers graciously taught her the routine over to the side. However, her director called me this evening and inquired whether Heather was still sick. She had not been herself and seemingly, had not enjoyed practice.

Heather explained to me that she had just been tired. "How could this be?" I asked her. She had gone to bed on time last night and had actually eaten a healthy lunch today (which, unfortunately, to my understanding, is not always a daily event for teenage girls). Not accepting her explanation, I told her that she must battle fatigue with enthusiasm and that she needed to set a wonderful example for the rest of the team.

At 2 o'clock this morning I awoke and began to read Willard Tate's <u>Learning to Love</u>. As I read on, I discovered that I was presently unhappy with myself. I realized that I had been extremely selfish. What I had really wanted from Heather was for her to make ME look good in front of my colleagues. As I read a certain passage, "Father Forgets", I began to sob. I had been too hard on my child.

Now, I must critically evaluate myself in my new role as "Drill Team Mom." One of my main problems is that I am a "mother" figure in more ways than one. My daughter's director, not too long ago, was the captain of the college team that I direct. As a director, she has continued to call me for advice and support as she did when she had been captain. That role I revel in and cherish; anyone would. But the "real" mom role is the more difficult and trying of the two.

My experience seems to be much the same as that of a father who has his own business. When his son decides to join the business, he must feel tremendously proud and honored. However, an element of anxiety exists amongst those feelings as well. He doesn't want his son to make any of the mistakes that he has made. But the son has not had the benefit of acquired experience and unless he is allowed to fall on his face a few times, he won't learn to appreciate all that he has.

I don't want Heather to make any mistakes either, but I've come to realize that those mistakes are a necessary part of life.

So...I'm going to let go, I really am. Well, I'll try it tomorrow and see how it works. If not---STOP!!! I've got to think positively. It won't be easy, but I'm going to give it my best shot to strike a balance between being a drill team director and a drill team mom.

But I do know one thing---I'm going to tell Heather that I am sorry, and ask her forgiveness. And then I'll start over again and be the best Drill Team Mom I can possibly be.

Sandy Hinton

Buck Up!

"Buck up"—" to spring up with a quick plunging leap."

"Buck up"- when I first heard that phrase from my director I thought that she was talking about riding a horse or something. I was a clueless new member on the Silsbee High School Drill Team and I had much to learn.

I will never forget the week of practice before Homecoming. That Friday night we were to perform our high kick routine before the Homecoming crowd—students, faculty, alumni and all. To prepare for the big event, we had performance tryouts the Tuesday before, and I was the only new member who made the cut. I felt great pride in that distinction, but I quickly learned that that same pride could lead to downfall as well. It was with that downfall I first learned the meaning of the phrase, "buck up."

Thursday afternoon, November 6, 1998. It was about forty degrees—what we southeastern Texans consider 'freezing.' The chosen got in line and began to practice. No sooner did we start then we had to stop, once because my toes weren't pointed, the next time because I wasn't smiling, and again because I was hunching in order to make my kicks seem higher.

The old members and our director were becoming extremely frustrated, and needless to say, so was I. As soon as I got angry at myself, things only got worse. By allowing myself to get angry and to have a bad attitude, my mind and body clammed up. The mistakes kept on coming.

During a water break, my director pulled me to the side and told me that I had to "buck up." There were those same two words again, except that when I heard them this time around, I knew just what she meant. She certainly wasn't talking about riding a horse. She was referring to the attitude and the performance that I owed not only to my teammates and to her, but to myself as well. With this warning and encouragement in mind, I was able to get through the tortuous practice that I thought would never come to an end. I was even able to leave with the feeling that I had given it my all.

That Friday night, we performed and marched off the field towards a crowd that was on its feet cheering for *us*. It was the greatest feeling in the world—knowing that we had given it our all and that all our hard work had paid off. Even better was seeing the look on our director's face. It's funny how a look can say it all. Her look told us that she was proud of our awesome performance. From that look, we knew how she felt; she didn't have to tell us; but she did anyway. Her pride in us meant more to me than the standing ovation we received from the crowd.

"Buck up"—Webster describes it as "to spring with a quick plunging leap; -said of a horse or a mule." In my own words—pushing yourself until you feel you no longer can, and then pushing yourself that much more.

Holly McGraw

A Coach's Pride

There is some place where your specialties can shine. Somewhere that difference can be expressed. It's up to you to find it, and you can.
~David Viscott

I was on the dance team my last two years of high school. When it was time for me to graduate I found it extremely difficult to leave. So I planned on coming back every so often to assist.

Once in college, I tried out for a spot on the cheerleading squad. I was overjoyed when I discovered that I had made the team. However, my joy was overshadowed when I was informed that my high school dance team would be losing a coach. Although busy with my new team, I assured my former high school dance director that I would be glad to help out until she found a replacement.

That summer with my former dance team proved rewarding. The team members became "my girls." I took them in and taught them from scratch. I connected with them in a way that I never thought possible. I began to dread the end of the summer when I would have to relinquish my place in their lives, and their places in mine. However, before summer's end, the head coach offered me the permanent position as the choreographer/coach. I was so excited at the prospect of actually having the chance to stay with "my girls", but I also knew that I would not have the time both to coach and to pursue my own cheerleading endeavor. I was faced with a tough decision; I had to choose between the two things that I loved most.

Coaches are there to offer support and encouragement. There have been times in my life when a coach seemed to be the only person that cared about me. Each one of them, at one time or another, had assured me that I could make any dream reality if I worked hard enough. The thought of having that kind of effect on just one girl helped me to decide. I would teach "my girls" the wonders of dance.

Being their coach has not been the easiest job. It has been stressful and frustrating. My efforts sometimes seem to go unappreciated. It's difficult to be firm and caring at the same time. Some nights I leave practice asking myself if I had made the right decision.

"My girls" performed for the first time the other night. I watched as they gave it their all. They were beautiful and graceful. I saw the spark; I felt their passion. My heart melts to think that I had any part of inspiring it. That night they shone like stars and I knew that I had indeed made the right decision.

But this story is not in praise of myself. This story is about them. The attachment between a coach and a team is so strong. I took the job with hopes that I would have a positive effect on at least one person's life. Instead, they each have changed my life. I realize that they love me in their own special way. They constantly push themselves beyond their limits to make me proud. There are many times that I have cried tears of pride.

What they need to know is that they are my heart and soul. Anderson County High School's dance team gives me the will to breathe and the strength that everyone needs. I have a feeling that every coach has a moment in time when they feel they are the proudest coach in the whole world. At least I know I do; it happens every day.

Christina Wells

Love, Tori

"…Talk to me, and I will remember your words…"

As an assistant, I coached my daughter's cheerleading squad for two years. During the second season, the other coach and I had tremendous problems seeing eye-to-eye. Rather than set a poor example of sportsmanship, I chose instead to leave the squad.

For closure I wrote a note to the girls explaining that my departure was for the best. The day after my resignation, while picking my daughter up from practice, one of the girls stopped me and gave me a letter.

I have kept this letter in my purse and have often shared it with others. When I am down or am at odds with my daughter, I read it. Written from the heart of a thirteen-year old cheerleader, this is the best compliment and greatest encouragement a coach could ever receive. Because of it, I found the courage to come back to the team…

Dear Mrs. Auriene,

As I write this letter to you, I cry. They are not tears of physical pain, but rather tears of emotional pain and sorrow.

I have read your letter over several times now, and I'm sorry. I'm sorry if I have done anything to contribute to your quitting the squad. The squad has come to a fork in the road, the same fork that we have encountered many times before. And I hope to God that we may take the right path and not follow in the fatal footsteps of the past.

I have seen many coaches come and go and have seen our squad fail, but through it all, I believe that our squad has built a rope. Our rope, not of twine nor string nor any other frail objects, is made of a substance that will outlive time- - friendship.

Today while on a school field trip, I was greeted by some of my squad mates. Kristen, Carlene, and Le Anne didn't seen to care what their friends and passersby thought of them, they pushed their way to the front and hugged me warmly.

I guess that the point of this story is that I hope you will always consider me a friend and will always greet me warmly with a hug and not feel embarrassment that you have known me. I also hope there will be a place in your heart for me, because I know there will always be one in mine for you. I ask you now to please come to games and competitions and an occasional practice- don't forget the band-aids!

Thank you for all the time that you have put in. ....I'll remember................Smile at me, and I'll remember your face, young or old. Talk to me, and I'll remember your words, wise or not. Listen to me, and I'll remember you forever, no matter what.

Love, Tori

Peggy Auriene

The Coach

"How can you have a beautiful ending without first making beautiful mistakes?"

I had only meant to be a volunteer. A helper. An assistant. I never had intentions of being *the coach*. After all, I was the mother of twin sons. I had never reared a girl. In fact, I had never spent much time with them. But there I was, the last week of school, handing out squad assignments with the soon-to-be-extinct *real* cheerleading coach.

I had never experienced anything like it before. Girls squealing. Girls sobbing. Moms yelling. I went home in shock, wondering what I had gotten myself into. A week later, I was informed that the coach had quit, and I was left for the summer with thirty-two adolescent girls.

Over the summer we practiced. Oh, how we practiced. Some nights, I went home feeling shell-shocked. How was I ever going to teach them to maintain straight arms? Were those toe touches ever going to look like something more than jumping jacks? What in the world was I doing with thirty-two 7th and 8th grade girls?

Just before the start of the school year, the squad was asked to help with "Back-to-School" night. It was the first time that season that the cheerleaders were to wear their uniforms. As they paraded in, wearing blue and red hair ribbons and squeaky-clean sneakers, I was overcome with emotion.

Somehow, those gangly arms and legs had grown stiff and strong. The jumps were higher than I had ever seen them. The stunt went off without a hitch. I had done it. No, they had done it. I was so proud of them.

And when the night was over, I cried all the way home.

Judy Paluso

The Coach's Room

If you're losing sleep and you have a knot in your stomach, that means you are probably doing your job. ~Bill Walsh

Warning: 12 signs that show you have entered the vicinity of your coach's room at summer camp...

1.   Room does not smell like pizza.

2.   No dirty clothes lying on the floor.

3.   No stuffed animals on the bed.

4.   No pictures of boyfriends pasted on the wall.

5.   Radio tuner is set to the "Oldies" station.

6.   Drapes are always closed.

7.   Room is quiet.

8.   Large bottles of nerve pills, muscle relaxers and aspirin are on the dresser.

9.   Young people cannot be found within ten feet of entrance.

10. If any music can be heard coming from room, there is no difficulty understanding the lyrics...

11. and the singers' names are composed of two words.

12. The only thongs to be found in the room are those worn on the feet.

Doneeta Kallal

When She Thought No One Was Watching

For Coach Melissa Colon

A good coach will make his players see what they can be rather than what they are. ~Ara Parasheghian

When she thought no one was watching

She smiled at what she saw.

She saw in us potential

That was little more than raw.

When she thought no one was watching

She stayed up countless nights

To invent the perfect stunt

That we'd perform under those lights.

When she thought no one was watching

Inside we saw her dying

Each time one of us got hurt

And stifled back the crying.

When she thought no one was watching

She gave us so much more

Than most coaches ever dream of

Just to see us soar.

When she thought no one was watching,

But believe me that we were,

Each of us became a better one

'Cause we were watching her.

Megan Lambart

That Friend I Call My Coach

Flatter me, and I may not believe you. Criticize me, and I may not like you. Ignore me, and I may not forgive you. Encourage me, and I may not forget you. ~William Arthur

I finally learned

What life is all about.

The secret of success

Comes hard no doubt.

I trained, I sweated,

I ached, I cried

And found out I got better

Each time I tried.

I was pushed, yelled at

And preached at too.

But the more that this happened

The more I grew.

"You can be anything

you want to be!"

This voice kept shouting

Out to me.

Yet, who can I blame

For such a daring approach—

THAT GENERAL

THAT COUNSELOR

THAT FRIEND I CALL

MY COACH.

Author Unknown

The Coach's *Real* Manual

Ingenuity, plus courage, plus work, equals miracles. ~Bob Richards

When you took on running a squad little did you realize the host of things that maybe should have been on your C.V. for the job. Surely all you had to do was get some girls together, obtain uniforms, practice some cheers, then off the first game. Or was it...

Your initial tryout was really a recruiting session, and none of the keen applicants who arrived had ever seen cheerleading before. Perhaps you were hoping there was at least one who had done this sort of thing before and knew some material to use. If this sounds familiar, take heart, you are not alone. This is the way that most squads were formed.

Here are some of the principal skills needed, none of which appear in the manuals. You will require the wisdom of Solomon, the patience of a saint, the understanding of a social worker, a sense of clairvoyance, and the ability to do twelve things simultaneously. As a friend, a counselor, a taxi driver, a choreographer, a PR officer, a diplomat and a secretary, you absolutely must have a little zip-up bag, for all those items of jewelry they were specifically told not to bring.

Being an out-of-school activity you will learn how to book halls and transport, and be instantly able to rebuild all your routines at the last moment because someone had extra studies, illness, Saturday jobs, obligations to visiting relatives, auditions, changes in shift work, or was grounded.

It is essential that you have plenty of cassettes, batteries, First Aid supplies, hair grips, poster paints, brushes, insurance, soda, Runts, shoe laces, sleeping bags, a considerate phone company and twenty-five hours a day of free time. Besides spending many a late night sewing uniforms, you tend to focus on the next game and your TV becomes monopolized by cheerleading videos. Practice becomes a time without time where decibels know no limit. You plan an ambitious schedule on a budget that would make a piggy bank wince - and succeed.

Do not be alarmed, this is quite normal, for there is something else important they probably forgot to tell you - the sheer fun of it all! These high-spirited extroverts may drive you to distraction with their enthusiasm and noise but they have become very special to you...

Developing character and maturity, pride of purpose, with confidence in themselves and in each other. Working as a team doing something positive and worthwhile. When they come off the field after a game and joy radiates in every direction, when they sing spirit songs after that hard-fought win. When the crowd yells back, and when Head Coach thanks them for their efforts and dedication to the team...

Sharing every moment of achievement and with memories to last there can be few activities as fulfilling and rewarding. Except for that piggy bank - but then there's always the next fund-raiser to keep us going.

Bob Kiralfy/ British Cheer Association

Unexpected Thanks

"There are little eyes upon you and they're watching night and day."

As a cheer camp instructor, each summer I was blessed with the opportunity not only to help kids improve their cheerleading skills, but to also teach them how to become role models and leaders in their communities.   Sometimes I was also fortunate enough to make an unexpected impact on their lives.

Although it was my fourth year with the cheer company, it was my first year as Head Instructor. Being Head Instructor meant that I was in charge of planning the schedule, organizing the instructional staff, preparing advisor meetings, making sure the facilities and stages were all set up, and smoothing out any problems that arose along the course of the four-day camp. Needless to say, I was unable to avoid the butterflies that fluttered in my stomach intermittently throughout the week.

The third night of camp was usually the most exciting. After working hard in the sun for three long days, we always liked to finish off the nightly activities with some fun activities. They deserved that on their last night. After the conclusion of our All-Star tryouts, perhaps the most stressful event at camp, the cheerleaders, the instructional staff, and particularly the Head Instructor, actually got a chance to exhale and relax.

At this particular camp, the seven female staff members, including myself, did a skit that we had prepared for all the kids. Then the male "staffers" did a performance to a mix that they created, imitating The Backstreet Boys, N'Sync, and several other popular male artists. The kids went nuts. It was a blast!

After all the excitement and goofing around, I was ready to dismiss the kids for the night when I felt a gentle tap on my arm. I turned to see the sweet freckled face of the strawberry-blonde Emily, a pint-sized cheerleader from a small Christian junior high school, gazing up at me. She quietly and politely asked if her squad could borrow the stage for a minute. She requested that the staff all sit together in the front row.

Twelve nervous cheerleaders formed a single file line across the stage, each of them holding a wrinkled piece of paper. Curious as to what these angelic cheerleaders were about to do, for the first time in three days, three hundred-fifty cheerleaders were astonishingly silent. Breaking the silence, two girls approached the microphone and began to sing. Giggling and reading from the crumpled sheets in their hands, at first their timid voices were hard to hear, but they slowly became very clear.

They were singing the song "Pretty Woman." I listened a little longer and it shortly dawned on me that they had rewritten the words. I felt my face become flushed as I realized they were singing about me! My eyes welled up with tears as they continued,

"Pretty woman, a true beauty queen; Pretty woman, just like I want to be; Pretty woman, Oh mercy, mercy, mercy me! Pretty woman, dance awhile; Pretty woman, cheer awhile; Pretty woman, Lynette with her barrette."

I adjusted the fore-mentioned barrette that I always wore in my hair and wiped the tear that had just run down my cheek as the next two girls took their place at the microphone. They began to sing a song about Mike, one of the other instructors. The whole camp listened intently, everyone with a smile and some even with tears. When each pair of girls had finished their song, the next two would sing. They had written a song about each of the members of my staff, highlighting personal and positive things that each of them had done throughout the week. Some were comical, and all were sweet. It was apparent that the girls had put a great deal of thought and effort into this performance. When finished, they thanked us for doing what we do and for helping them to become better cheerleaders.

That night I received one of the greatest rewards one could ever long for. I, along with my wonderful staff, had served as good role models and positive influences, and had made a difference in the lives of those children. Whenever I get caught up in the hustle and bustle of the business side of things, I simply remind myself of Emily and her cheer squad.

Whether we realize it or not, as instructors, there are always little eyes watching us and looking to us to be those positive examples. And sometimes we are privileged enough to have someone tell us just what we mean to her.

Lynette Weaver

Heart and Soul

"A coach is someone special who thinks of those in need. She brings a bit of sunshine with every caring word and deed."

Ever since I can remember, dancing has been my life. At parties, I have always been the first to jump on the dance floor and get the crowd going. I just put my heart and soul into the music and let my body go. That's the great thing about dancing—it comes from within. It's my passion.

During my junior high and freshman years, cheerleading was the only activity available to girls that related to dancing. It was not quite what I was looking for and not exactly what I wanted to do, but hey, at least I got the chance to somewhat dance. I cheered for three years of my life.

One day, at the end of my freshman year, I saw posters hanging all over school announcing the upcoming poms' tryouts. This was it—finally I could try out for something that I really loved! My best friend Trisia, already on the team, helped me out with the basics. We worked hard, and I made it. Piece of cake, I thought. Well, after tryouts, the real work came into play. It was time for practice…

I had taken Greek dancing my whole life.   I was a maniac on the dance floor. But boy, was I in for a surprise! The dancing that they did in Poms did not consist of the dancing that was second-nature to me. I mean, this was serious business! Foette, double, axel—what were these words, more importantly, what kind of moves were they??

I thought I had this dancing stuff down like the pros until I had to learn all these new technical moves. I had never done a turn or gone down in the splits. Seriously now, how many people have you seen getting down with foettes in the middle of a club? Ummm…none!

Poms was a totally new experience. Being a new member of a squad with a bunch of veteran and talented girls was difficult. I felt like such a loser. Just watching what the rest of them could do made me so self-conscious. They were so intimidating!

I just wanted to give up. I tried at practice but it did not seem like I was getting anywhere. After a while, the captains started making easier routines just to accommodate us newer members. Not that we didn't improve—we attended two summer camps to improve our technical skills. We survived daily double practices. We all worked really hard.

And then one day, while preparing for competition, I injured my leg. After that I lost any semblance of hope. Not only did my injury cause me pain, but it also set me further back from the others. Luckily, I recovered enough to compete with the team. Okay, so I wasn't as technically able as the others, but I had proved to them that I could perform well enough to compete.

As luck would have it though, I again injured my leg performing at competition! This time I was not so lucky, and had to sit out for several performances. Now I was really discouraged.

My teammates were great. They were very supportive. However, when it came to crunch time, they couldn't help me with what I needed the most—to catch up to them technically.

"Take it home," they advised me. "You'll get it if you just practice harder."

But I didn't even have the basics down enough to take it home. How could I perfect my double when I was still struggling with the concept of spotting?

Then …a ray of light. Kelly, our assistant coach, believed in me a little more than anyone else did, including myself. She took the time to show me how to do all the technical stuff correctly. She showed me little tricks on how to perfect form and execution. When she told me to "take it home and practice," I could, because I now knew what I was doing!

She helped me reach my goals. She gave me hope and the enthusiasm to again attempt to "take it home." Within a couple weeks Kelly had me doing doubles and leaps. By the end of the year, I received the award for "Most Improved."

This meant a lot to me. Not only did that trophy belong to me, but also to Kel. Since then, I have gone on to learn some pretty incredible moves and to become head captain of our team. I thank Kelly for all that I have learned, have accomplished and will continue to accomplish in dance.

Gina Giannakopoulos

What Will They Remember?

Friendship consists in forgetting what one gives, and remembering what one receives. **~Dumas the Younger**

What will they remember

When the last trophy is won?

Will it be the wood and metal

Or the laughter, tears, and fun?

What will they remember

From all your coaching days?

The way you yelled and pleaded

Or the magic of your praise?

What will they remember:

The music, chants and cheers?

Will it be the stunts and jumps

Or belief that conquers fears?

Just what are the values

That glow with practice sweat?

That survive beyond performing,

That transcend, "What'd ya get?"

Teamwork is a value

I'm confident will endure.

Sportsmanship and leadership,

Unified and pure.

Belief is a value

That stands the test of time.

Faith in good transcending

The vision of love sublime.

Courage is a value

That daily will sustain.

Free from fear, undaunted

With confidence we will reign.

Friendship is a value

That gives our life a lift

Connecting us through time and space:

It's our most treasured gift.

What will they remember?

I've often asked myself.

Will it be my smiles and hugs

Or a trophy on the shelf?

So when you go to practice,

And sometimes curse the day,

Remember the heart of coaching

Is what you do and what you say.

Treat everyone with kindness

And create a sacred place:

Where you as coach and mentor

Can see greatness on every face.

In the spotlight of competition

In the heat of the judge's glare,

Remember to instill pride and passion.

Remember to show you care.

Linda Rae Chappell

Good Bye From Your Coaches

"Never say goodbye, say farewell."

Thank you, Cheerleaders, for your very special smiles

Our (mascot) friendship circle unites us across the miles.

We share a special commitment, our love is strong and dear.

The feelings we have shared together last throughout the year.

We know you work real hard, and practices are sometimes tough.

But for what we feel for you, we just can't give enough.

We want so much to help you be the best that you can be--

To know each other closely and to work in harmony.

We hope you understand us and know us as your friends.

Hold fast to special memories for our friendship never ends.

Thank you most of all for simply saying YES!

You worked to reach your goals and your spirit is the best.

We love you all so much, you warm and touch our hearts.

Your spirit stays within us even when we are apart.

So take this simple message and share it wherever you go.

Be yourself and share your love because your coaches love you so!

Linda Rae Chappell

hit it!
Ready...hit it!"

To Every Cheerleader

Example is not the main thing influencing others. It is the only thing.
~Albert Schweitzer

There are little eyes upon you

And they're watching night and day.

There are little ears that quickly take in every word you say.

There are little hands all eager to do anything you do.

And a little girl who is dreaming of the day

She'll be like you.

You're the little girl's idol;

You're the wisest of the wise.

In her little mind

About you no suspicions ever rise.

She believes in you devoutly,

Holds that all you say and do

She will say and do in your way

When she's a grown-up

Just like you.

There's a wide-eyed little girl who believes you're always right;

And her ears are always open

And she watches day and night!

You are setting an example

Every day in all you do

For the little girl

Who is waiting to grow up to be like you!

Author Unknown

Imagine

Image creates desire. You will what you imagine. ~ **J.G. Gallimore**

You walk into the Salem Civic Center lobby. You wait with your squad in the check-in line, where the other spirit groups ahead of you are being admitted into the Division III NCAA championship game.

Walking down the cement steps, you proudly don your 'NCAA Visitor' button on your garnet warm-up jacket. Turning the corner into the gymnasium, you are suddenly overcome with the size of the arena. The ceiling is incredibly high. The rafters reach towards the sky. The rows of blue seats seem infinite…

The court is empty. The freshly mopped, lacquered floor glistens, seemingly waiting impatiently, for the scuffs to be made by a multitude of basketball shoes. Off the floor, the team managers pour water into cups from a large blue container. The sound of ripping brings you around to the here and now, as the athletic trainer wraps your bases' ankles and wrists.

You notice the coaches contemplating their surroundings. You can almost see the clockwork whirring in their heads. The press people are busy setting up computers and radio equipment. The arena reverberates with the faint chatter from all the people preparing the gym. The area is thick with anticipation.

The court is a blank slate. The basketball players will inscribe their story on it. Their story will be the first of its kind in school history. Keeping this in mind you are determined to lead the crowd in a way that will motivate your team like never before. You are proud of your school and yourself.

Feeling full of spirit, you hope the other team has a good game but you know where your loyalty lies. Contemplating the very possible win, you look around to see your squad mates happily grinning as well. In a blur of garnet and white, your team enters the court for warm up. The crowd roars. Dark orange balls seem to herd the players in a controlled formation.

The buzzer sounds and the team lines up. The announcer speaks on behalf of sportsmanlike conduct. He introduces the National Anthem. A male opera student from Emory and Henry, with a beautifully trained voice, sings as the crowd listens reverently.

As he hits the last notes, the crowd explodes with whistles and screams. The presentation of the players brings on boos from half the gym and cheers from the other. This alternates many times as each starting player from both teams are introduced.

You lead the crowd in several simple chants, such as "H-S-C" and "Defense XX". Another squad member takes the initiative and uses a megaphone. Her voice loudly exits the plastic cone. A shower of garnet, silver and white pom pons shakes around you. Prepping for a jump, you feel the support your mid-cut Nikes™ lend to your ankles. You execute a perfect toe touch with flexible legs and strong hip flexors as they rotate flawlessly in the air.

The captain turns to you and informs you that you will fly during the first full time-out's stunt. The others will dance to the song around your stunt. You feel excited to show the crowd how hard you have worked on your extension with a twist cradle. Your smile widens.

Time flies by and suddenly you hear the ref.'s shrill whistle. Time for the first time-out. Is it a full or a 20 second? You quickly look towards the ref. to see his arms displayed in a T. You look at your captain and she repeats the signal. It's a full time-out.

The band starts in with the "Hey" song. Eager and excited, you run onto the court. As your breath quickens, you tell yourself to remain in control. You successfully do so as you set up for the stunt.

You place your hands on your two bases' shoulders and feel the back base securely grab your waist. You hear the counts being exclaimed loudly over the din of the music. "Extension 1-2." You take a small prep onto your toes. "Down-up!" You bend your knees and jump upwards. Your calves ripple with energy. As your legs extend, your arms lock out and you distribute all your weight evenly over your bases. Like a balanced ball, your body poses--bottom up and back straight.

As you hear the next "down" sounded out, you horizontally aim your feet into your bases' hands and bend your arms. "Up," the back base shouts as she uses your rear end as leverage to shoot you upwards. At that same instance you look forward and explode through your triceps.

You are now standing firmly on only your two bases' hands. They are holding you with their arms fully extended over their heads. You squeeze with your inner thighs and pull up through your torso and shoulders. Their hands and your feet feel as solid as a concrete floor.

You have absolute faith in their ability to support you and to catch you. All thoughts of falling are absent from your mind. With simple arm motions and a smile, you direct the crowd, encouraging them to join in your efforts to support the team. You welcome the sound of the crowd yelling along with the band and the roar of the opposing fans yelling with their own cheerleaders. The arena seems to be in auditory chaos, but you now only hear your bases' commands.

You anticipate a twist cradle and instantly envision it in your mind. As you mentally create the image, you physically perform everything picture perfect. "Twist cradle 1-2 down-up." On "up" you pull your pelvis up towards your arms extended above your head.

Looking over your left shoulder, you see your back base. Simultaneously, you wrap your arms to your left hip and feel the spin begin. As you reach the bottom of the fall you unfold and concentrate on keeping your ankles close to one another and your body tight.

The three bases catch and absorb you. You feel the burn of your uniform scraping against your back, but ignore the pain. Everyone is smiling including you and your three bases. You have just hit the cleanest stunt in your cheerleading career.

Sarah Kingsley Foley

Explosion

"Cheerleading is life. The rest is just details."

Why do our lives begin on the wooden floors of the local high school

And end on the blue mats in Dallas and Jacksonville?

Why do we live half our lives at the nearest gymnastics academy, open school gym

or even the parking lot...

and live the other half packed in ice and jammed into knee braces?

Why do we spend fifteen to twenty hours a week--

Smiling alike, sounding alike and walking alike?

It's not because we are the prettiest or the most popular girls in school.

It's not because we want to grow up to be professional cheerleaders.

And it's not because we think the uniforms are cute.

If those were the reasons, we could never be All-Stars.

There are no guts, heart or glory found in the reasons above.

We cheer because we love the gym floor.

Even when we fall to its hard gleam.

We cheer because we don't mind the ice, air cast, knee brace,

Pain.

These are just the preliminaries of competition and our rewards.

We cheer because the explosion of power and talent

On the blue mats of Dallas, Jacksonville, Orlando and Atlanta

Is beyond any beauty pageant, popularity contest, or football game.

We see your awe, amazement, and pride from above our partners' heads.

We know what you really know, should know, or just don't want to know.

We cheer because we are more than just gymnastics.

We cheer because we are more than just dancing.

We cheer because we are more than just acrobatics.

We cheer because we are more than your average girl.

Jillian Kendall Gray

Cocktail Recipe

"I cheer, therefore I am."

Take two measures of Gatorade and Isostar and allow to dissolve slowly into 120 pounds of pure energy, premixed with equal quantities of dedication and enthusiasm.

Add spice, and the zest of a dozen Freshman peers. Any outside sour grapes can be taken with a pinch of salt.

Carefully blend in choreography, plyometrics, gymnastics, and camp ingredients. When set for into pyramids. Whisk up some fundraising power and pour into new uniforms.

Warm up thoroughly then allow to stand on sideline until crowd attendance rises. Fire up Spirit Gas Mark 9, light the blue touch paper and stand well clear.

Keep on the boil over a hot summer, top with a smooth icing of confidence, and garnish with smiles. Serve hot throughout season then transfer to Bowl.

Bob Kiralfy

C-H-E-E-R-L-E-A-D-E-R-S

It is not the position, but the disposition. ~J. E. Dinger

C aring
H elpful
E ager
E cstatic
R espectful
L oving
E fficient
A ccepting
D edicated
E lite
R eassuring
S pirited

Wendy Andry

C razy
H ardworking
E xcellent
E ntertaining
R eliable
L eading
E nthusiastic
A thletic
D etermined
E nergetic
R eady to win
S pirited

Sarah Scoggins

Put Yourself In My Cheerleading Shoes

If you judge people, you have no time to love them. ~Mother Theresa

When I say the word 'cheerleader', what thoughts come to mind?

Go ahead and say them, I know some thoughts may not be kind.

Some things people say have the tendency to hurt,

Sometimes disrespectful and make me feel like dirt.

But if you listen closely, I'm sure that you will find,

I'm none of those things, at least not in my mind.

Cheerleading is a way to get involved in school.

It's not a way to become popular or cool.

Most cheerleaders are intelligent, not dumb at all.

And no, my favorite hobby is not shopping in the mall!

We practice many hours during the week.

We consider cheerleading a sport that is truly unique.

We support football, basketball, and volleyball too…

Without even a thought if we have support from you!

If I didn't wear the uniform you would clearly see,

I'm just a regular teenager—just plain old me!

So before you even know me, don't be quick to judge.

And because I have different interests, don't hold a grudge.

It's common in high school that you will find—

People with stereotypes, and it's hard to change their minds.

But put yourself in my cheerleading shoes

Just for a day.

And I know that you'll think twice

About the rude things you might say.

Elizabeth Stallard

A Bedside Prayer

"Cheerleaders are born, not made!"

Now I lay me down to rest,

I've tried my hardest and have done my best

To tumble, jump, dance and cheer

With the sharpest of motions and no trace of fear.

I know in the morning that my body will ache.

But for what I love

It's a price gladly paid!

Thank you God for making me strong,

With determination and commitment

When the practices were long.

And Lord,

If I should die before I wake,

I'll know I've shown the world

CHEERLEADERS ARE BORN, NOT MADE!

Author Unknown

Perfection

***Perfection is our goal, excellence will be tolerated.* ~J. Yahl**

High up in the arms of others,

Where trust and fear live within us flyers.

Smiling and sparkling as I play to the crowd,

Wishing and hoping—God don't let me fall.

It's my time to shine, showing off my stretch—

Squeeze, pull in, just pull off the rest!

Execution the sharpest, flexibility first-rate—

Now's the time for me to rotate!

My double full down is the hardest part yet-

Remember—be tight, be confident and I'll be all set!

The call is made and clearly heard, "1,2."

Double full down complete

That's perfection for you!!

Heather E. Ransom

My Megaphone

"It's more than just a game."

Cheerleading

The sport I love.

It's more than just a game.

It's more than standing on the sidelines, looking cute.

It's more than just wearing a short skirt and yelling.

It's boasting about my team with confidence and esteem

Using my megaphone.

When it's all over and we win the game

I proudly chant those eight powerful words:

"I'm so glad that I go to SHS."

Using my megaphone.

Cheerleading is life.

But I'd be nowhere without my megaphone.

I love this sport and

MY MEGAPHONE.

Christi Lee

Climber

"Cheerleader (n.): An ATHLETE who can jump, kick, toss, catch, stunt, tumble and fly!"

When the beating of my heart is the only sound.

When I'm scratched

Bruised

Dropped.

When I hit the ground.

When trust is hard to keep,

When the fears awaken

That should just sleep.

When my endurance starts to fade.

When I'm tired

Broken

Afraid.

When I look into anxious eyes,

When I feel success only in my mind,

When we stumble

And fall another time.

When I bleed

Scream

Cry.

What keeps me jumping in is

That moment

I get to fly.

Brigette Workman

Life As A Cheerleader

"Peace, Love, Cheer."

When I wake up in the morning,

I think about one thing--

Cheering for the players

At every football game.

Cheering on my team,

With the crowd of fans on their feet.

Cheering on the sidelines

Watching the other team get beat.

Yelling with spirit,

Clapping my hands,

Watching the excited faces

Of all the Panther fans.

We've scored another touchdown.

The crowd goes wild.

There is no getting around it--

We're ahead by a mile!

Doing my jumps

Flying high in the sky

The base comes to my rescue

The crowd lets out a huge sigh.

This is my life as a cheerleader.

It's fun as you can see.

This is my life as a cheerleader,

And it works for me!

Madison Carlton

Cheerleading Is...

"Let's hear it!"

Cheerleading is a way of life, shared by a chosen few.

It is working as a unit in everything you do.

Cheerleading is rivalry; the competition makes you strong.

It is sharing secrets and tears, learning to get along.

Cheerleading is that ongoing drive to be the very best.

It is patience, perseverance, and very little rest.

Cheerleading is having poise and charm with every word you say.

It is total dedication twenty-four hours a day.

It is always being ready with encouragement or a smile.

Cheerleading is your chance to express your individual style.

Cheerleading is reaching out to comfort a sister who is sad;

It is defending each other in the good times and the bad.

Cheerleaders are always there whenever someone asks-

They treasure the present moment and let go of the past.

Cheerleading is a talent to be able to shine on cue.

It is hiding the pain and anguish that if only people knew.

Cheerleaders after all, are real people that sometimes get down

but when they're in the spotlight, they must never put on a frown.

Cheerleaders are actresses, always ready to go.

That is why it is important for all the world to know--

Not every girl can be a cheerleader; it takes a special kind.

Cheerleaders are full of life and a little bit out of their mind.

Reprinted from AICMMagazine

Cheer With My Heart

The first thing is to love your sport. Never do anything to please someone else. The desire has to be yours. **~Peggy Fleming**

There are many great things about the sport of cheer.

Some of them I love; some of them I fear.

I fear the injury, muscle pains and the aches

But I would not stop cheering for any sake.

For I have grown to love this sport.

And if I do not give my all, I am not the only one who comes up short.

I have not only myself to think about,

But my many teammates who expect me to help out.

For without any one of us, the team is not the same.

I know that I never want to be the one that shoulders the blame.

So everyday that I stand up and I cheer, I will give it my all

For if we all do this, we simply cannot fall.

Beside the pom pons, megaphones, and spirit sticks,

Cheerleading is more than just the jumps and the kicks.

Cheerleading is a part of me

For without it, I simply cannot be.

I will show spirit the best that I can

Because by believing in myself, I am my own #1 fan!

For the rest of my life, I do believe that cheerleading will always be dear to me.

Whether I am cheering for my teammates, school, family or myself

I will always cheer with all I have in me.

For spirit, love, and success not only comes from cheerleading but from life itself.

I know now and forever that cheerleading will always play a part,

And that through all the trials and tribulations of life,

I will cheer with my heart!!

Carrie Tharp

On Track

"To cheer or not to cheer? What a stupid question!"

As I step upon the track

All the memories take me back

To the games and half-times gone by.

When I leave I almost cry.

For reasons others might not plainly see--

The many friends and good times behind me.

The end of a season, the end of a sport--

A sport not acknowledged as a sport of that sort.

All the happiness there is inside…

Still people called us names, yet we had no reason to hide--

We were there for ourselves, not to make others proud.

They thought we were stupid, with our heads in the clouds.

But much too often people did wrongly see.

"Cause most were good students, the best we could be.

Cheerleaders can be ever so stereotyped—

Ditzy and care-free, always wrong never right.

But as I stand thinking back on everything

I have an idea; that little bell rings.

Maybe they're jealous? Though there's really no reason.

But I'll do it again; you'll see me next season.

Mallory Morse

A Cheerleader's Prayer

Unless I had the spirit of prayer, I could do nothing. ~Charles G. Finney

Lord, please give me a glimmer of hope

When things get tough and I've had enough.

Lord please give me the confidence to try,

The will to believe, to understand failure, and to find the way to achieve.

Lord grant me a smile that is genuine and true

When I am anxious, upset, or feeling blue.

Help me to understand why that extra push is sometimes just what I need—

To continue to be strong, and to support me when I need to succeed.

Give me the love for others when they try to strive.

Help me to use patience as my motivating drive.

Guide me as a soaring bird that takes to the wing.

Because I need your direction Lord,

For all these things.

Sylvia S. Mullins

The Thank You Poem

"To each one of us friendship has a different meaning. For all of us it is a gift."

Cheerleaders, you each have a special way

Of smiling from the heart.

Your dedication is outstanding.

Your leadership sets you apart.

We share a bond of friendship

That transcends the spoken word.

We know we care for each other.

We can talk and we are heard.

Sometimes I make mistakes,

But I am trying all the while.

I want to do my best for you.

I'll go the extra mile.

Please know that you can count on me

If you need some place to go.

I'm here if you need me

When you're sad or feeling low.

I want only the best for you.

Keep reaching to be Number One!

I know that you can do it.

Your potential has just begun.

And so with the end of the season

You give my heart a lift.

Our very special friendship

Is my most cherished gift.

Linda Rae Chappell

just dance...

Breathe it, live it, love it...dance it!"

This Girl Is A Dancer!

***Dance is the only art in which we ourselves are the stuff of which it is made.* ~Ted Shawn**

She has class and charm, more than the rest.

Her positive attitude makes her the best--

A well-rounded role model for kids to admire,

With a sparkle in her eyes that burns like fire.

Confidence and poise make her first-rate.

Talent and imagination you wish to emulate.

She is an outgoing girl who can handle a crowd,

An excellent student that makes family proud.

Discipline and dedication inspire her to succeed.

A responsible girl, who helps those in need.

She can be sexy, graceful or sharp as a knife.

This girl really knows where she is headed in life.

She has spirit and motivation and takes pride in her team.

She reaches for the stars and captures her dream.

Who possesses these credentials? I must know the answer!

Then I shouted out loud:

This girl is a **DANCER!!**

Autumn Marisa

Dance

And finally, there are those who convert the body into a luminous fluidity, surrendering it to the inspiration of the soul. ~Isadora Duncan

Standing motionless, in front of the crowd, waiting. As the music starts, her body stirs and glides across the floor, a swan on a pristine lake. Flowing through time, giving herself to the music, a solitary flower rustling in the wind. Leaping high in the air, her arms smooth and soft like down. Spinning and leaping, a lone swan searching, looking for others of her kind. As the music fades and the curtains close, the crowd stands and cheers loudly. She lifts her bowed head one last time and smiles. For she knows what ignites the flame within a dancer's heart and wherein lies the secret to happiness...

DANCE.

Emily Blacksmith

You Know You're a Dancer

Nothing so clearly and inevitably reveals the inner man than movement and gesture. **~Doris Humphrey**

You know you're a dancer when...

You measure music in terms of 8 counts.

You couldn't possibly imagine kicking someone or something without your toes pointed.

You've got better kicks than the punter on the football team.

You make up routines in the shower.

You do routines in your sleep.

You know the difference between poms and cheerleading.

You doodle formations rather than write notes in class.

Double sessions aren't just for football players.

You and your teammates share the same monthly cycle.

You know every word of the school song.

You break into dance every time you hear it.

Vaseline is your smile's best friend.

Facials aren't something you have done at the salon.

Your fingernails are always short (at least when you're 'in season').

'In season' —7 days a week, twelve months a year.

'Spot' doesn't refer to the dog in your first-grade reader.

Blochs aren't just toys for kids.

Your sharpness would make a drill sergeant proud.

When taking pictures, you exclaim, "5,6,7,8" rather than "Say cheese!"

It can take a lifetime to establish credibility, minutes to destroy it—two minutes, in fact.

Half-time is when the real fun begins!

Sue Ann Kawecki

I Am a Funny Girl Who Dances

I do everything I know how in a dance. ~Twyla Twarp

I am a funny girl who dances.

I wonder why we are here.

I hear sweet music all night and all day.

I see life being lived to the fullest.

I want happiness for all.

I am a funny girl who dances.

I pretend to get away from it all.

I feel happy with friends and family.

I touch hearts, shedding a little love light...

I worry about my earth.

I cry over hatred.

I am a funny girl who dances.

I understand feelings.

I say I can be a good person.

I dream of dancing all over the country.

I try to give to others.

I hope all people will find each other in heaven.

I am a funny girl who dances.............

Angelina Palmer

Just Dance

"Don't think; just dance!"

Sometimes I come home from practice only to complain to my mom. "Mom, poms takes up too much of my time. I am sick of practicing four to seven days a week!" or "Poms was too hard today. I am soooo sore!"

She patiently listens to me gripe about how much more time I would have to do things if I weren't on the team. She always reminds me of those others who have tried out but did not make it and would love to have my spot on the squad. I constantly shrug it off because I figure that if people actually knew how consuming poms really was, they wouldn't try out in the first place.

During a rare hiatus from poms, I participated in a retreat. At one of the gatherings, I met a girl named Katie. It so happened that she attended a rival school. She shared this at one of the meetings whose sole purpose is to get members to share personal information with each other. I soon learned that Katie had much more to share.

During another one of our group gatherings, our leader started the meeting by revealing one of my personal life experiences. "For instance," she said, "Jennifer could share her pom squad's success at Nationals with us." I don't like to be the center of attention so I couldn't wait for the next person to share.

Well, we had already gone around the circle and it so happened that it was Katie's turn. Looking at all of us, she confided that she previously had brain tumors. Everyone sat, stunned.

Later, she told me that she envied me. She had been a dancer until the tumors got too advanced. The tumors caused her to lose her memory and made her unable to physically dance.

At an even later group meeting, we each told one another about one item that meant the world to each one of us. Katie told us about the treasured book her daddy had given to her when she no longer could dance. It was about a ballerina bunny.

Katie is someone I will always remember. She taught me not to take my abilities for granted. It's more important to be thankful for my abilities than to be proud of them.

It helps me to go out and dance and wow the crowd. It also helps me to sometimes remember to complain less when I come home from practice.

Author Unknown

Once Again

Dance till the stars come down from the rafters.
Dance, dance, dance till you drop. ~**W. H. Auden**

I try to talk, but find that I can't.

Unwillingly, I begin to pant.

The palms of my hands have become so sweaty.

I'm not quite sure if I am ready.

Will I dance well?

Then suddenly I am in front of the crowd.

As the lights begin to dim,

I twirl and dance for them.

The spotlight shines down upon me,

Dancing, I feel as if I'm floating on air.

My dance is done; fatigue envelops me.

The applause swells to an amazing roar.

I curtsey for my final pose and they applaud even more.

I bow once more and walk off, but then,

I suddenly wish I could dance once again.

Katie Rank

Tune In

The value of dance, its greatest values, is in the 'intangibles'. ~Ted Shawn

Tune in to the...

Value of time,

Success of perseverance,

Dignity of simplicity,

Worth of character,

Power of kindness,

Obligation of duty,

Influence of example,

Wisdom of economy,

Virtue of patience,

Improvement of talent, and

The joy of originating.

That's why we joined Drill Team.

Author Unknown

I Am A Dancer

Dance is an art that imprints on the soul. It is with you every moment; it expresses itself in everything you do. ~Shirley Maclaine

I am a dancer.

I smell it in my costume:

A mix of velvet, plastic sequins and Aqua Net.

I taste it in my lipstick,

Worn with sweat and anxious bites.

I hear it in the song we've heard a thousand times,

But still pulses through my veins as if it were the first.

I feel it in my stomach,

Churning with nervousness and excitement.

I see it in a thousand faces,

Smiling at every kick and turn of our routine.

I know it when I am sitting in class,

Tapping my feet under the desk...

Or when I am taking a shower,

Performing for my shampoo bottle.

I believe it as I walk onto the floor,

With my chin held high and my heart filled with pride.

I am a dancer.

Katie Dalton

No One Knows Like A Dancer Knows

"Socrates learned to dance when he was seventy because he felt that an essential part of himself had been neglected."

No one knows like a dancer knows

What it takes to win.

It takes practice, hard work, dedication,

And a feeling that comes from within.

A feeling that one has tried her hardest

Yet knows she will try even more.

A feeling that no one can be better than you

And that no team has been better before.

No one knows like a dancer knows

How much it hurts to lose.

To feel that all your long hard work

Hasn't been paid its dues.

A dancer knows like no one else

How important friendship is.

But to see twenty girls bonding is nothing new

Because it's all part of the "biz".

A dancer has seen happiness.

A dancer has been through pain.

A dancer has twirled in the sunlight.

A dancer has leaped in the rain.

A dancer will never attempt to give up.

Her best will always show.

She'll dance her story whenever she can

Because no one knows what a dancer knows.

Jonna Werner

A Comparison

"Dance isn't just about fancy footwork. It requires grace, discipline, and major muscles."

It's dancing and football I wish to compare—

Why they are similar and what they both share.

Between competitions, practices and games,

The work and the effort is simply the same.

A hundred and ten percent is required,

For athletes to give; there's no time to be tired.

The time, the patience, and endless devotion,

Commitment, and teamwork keep them in motion.

They reach and they strive to accomplish their goals,

Though all of the exercise takes a great toll.

They stretch and condition with no time to sit.

They work for perfection 'til everything clicks.

To practice a drill or run through a routine,

Over and over, for success is the dream.

They sweat and they strain as their bodies endure

The physical challenges both have in store.

They go through the motions, the jumps, turns and leaps—

On their knees, in the air, and back on their feet.

Both sports are demanding and require a need

For balance, coordination, strength and speed.

Though one is an art and the other a game,

The tough preparation is nearly the same.

In view of the work and the goals they fulfill,

Both football and dancing require the same skills!!

Beth C. Newton-Girard

A Little Goes A Long Way

"If you want to be the best, you have to give more!"

Smile… a little wider.

Point…a little harder.

Kick…a little higher.

Dance…a little tighter.

Ripple…a little faster.

Breathe…a little deeper.

Want…a little more

Than your opponents.

If you want to be the best…

You have to give more!

Submitted by Kathleen Daytner

Can't Breathe

Thousands of emotions well up inside me throughout the day. They are released when I dance. ~Abraham Lincony

Five six seven eight

Our fingers grasp where the silk meets the metal

We gaze into the eyes of our teammates

Assurance is gratifying.

Warm cheeks redden and gleam

Our smiles reach to the back of the bleachers

To the back of the walls

To the poster with our name.

Smiles forever radiating

Radiating

Radiating.

Precise movements

A single machine

Each count crawls under a deafening breath

5-6-7-squeeze and go

2-3-4, spin-and-turn: 6-7-8

Counting together

Telling the story of our wins and losses

Our fights

Our struggles and passions

A story of our song.

Spin-2 catch-3, down and up

Pushing each movement to the farthest of the gym

To the farthest watching spectator

Reaching into each of their hearts

Hearts of past coaches

Of our parents

To those that feel it.

Partnership

1-2-3-4

Locking arms and swaying

Completing a circle.

Our breath blends together

Our sweat bleeds into the floor

Into the courts and fields

Into the wood and earth

But still smiling

Still beaming

Still shining

Still

Silence

Breathe

Chins up

Eyes up

This is pride

This is Compassion

Friendship

Nirvana

Our lives and breath

Formed into silk, wood and sweat.

Cheyenne Barr

What Drill Team Means

Let your heart guide you. ~**The Land Before Time**

Being on the drill team is

What we love.

We reach for the stars,

Rather than say, "We could of..."

For most of us, the season

Lasts throughout the year.

And when it all comes to an end,

We're sadly sharing tears.

We create memories, friendships

And often share hugs.

Because it's our teammates

That we cherish and love.

Other than all the routines

That we make and we teach,

Together we learn to set goals

That we all strive to reach.

Drill teamers can do anything,

Even when the end seems out of sight.

If we just set our minds to it

We can do it, alright.

Anyone can dance

Just by moving their feet.

But a drill teamer feels the rhythm

From her head to her feet.

The dancing has to come

Straight from the heart.

It's always been there...

Right from the start.

Don't forget—

When you go out there

And repeatedly count to eight.

What drill team means to each one of us

And we won't be anything but great!

Deanna Johnson

There's a Hole in My Heart

These are the days we will remember. ~10,000 Maniacs

There's a hole in my heart in the shape of a pom.

It cannot be filled by my dad or my mom.

It cannot be filled by a comforting friend.

It will never be filled because this is the end.

It's the end of an era, the end of a season.

And it's very hard to think of a reason

For me to be settled, for me to be calm.

There's a hole in my heart in the shape of a pom.

No more performing for standing ovation.

No more pep talks about inspiration.

There will be no more practices crammed in the hall,

Not for me anymore, but I did have a ball.

Four years of my life that have shaped who I am

As a person, a dreamer, a leader, a friend.

So put that behind me. It's time to move on,

But there's a hole in my heart in the shape of a pom.

To all of you seniors, I hope you're not crying.

And to you freshman, I would be lying

If I said I'm not jealous, through all these tears,

Of you, because you have got three more years...

To be in pompon. So make the most of it.

Enjoy every moment and just know that you love it.

One day you're a pommer. The next, that's old news.

You'll wake up and discover that you have the blues.

You'll always remember those times that we had.

Some we were smiling; others were sad.

You'll tell your children when you are a mom

That there's a hole in your heart in the shape of a pom.

Megan Lambart

A Healing Power

Birth…and death…for all (of these) the dance is needed. ~**Curt Sachs**

July 23, 1999. The day my life changed. It didn't change because I had made the dance team or I had failed a class. That fateful day I was busy fulfilling my role as a UDA Head Instructor. While teaching a class at a summer camp, I was pulled to the side to take a phone call from my mom…

My father had had a second heart attack. To this day, I can replay the conversation with my mom, as if it were only two minutes ago. It's like a recording that plays over and over again—Dad had had another heart attack and I was to board a plane as soon as possible.

Three hours later, I walked off the plane at Logan Airport. I was expecting my boyfriend to pick me up—but was greeted by my mom instead. I should have known right then. Through her sunglasses, I could see the tears fall from her swollen eyes.

"He's gone." Two words and my life fell apart. At forty-nine, my father was dead. At nineteen, I was without a father.

It's now two months later, and to say life is hard is the understatement of the millennium. I have had to adjust to my new life. I am no longer Daddy's Little Girl; my brother is the man of the house; my mother is a single parent, a widow. But I am doing okay. I realize that this may sound cliché, but I am okay because I am a dancer.

Dance has always been my way to forget the outside world. Dancing has allowed me to escape into my OWN world where nothing else matters. I can let go and forget.

I'm okay not because I am a good dancer but because I have the heart of a dancer. I have a soul brimming with rhythm, just waiting for a stage and an audience. When I escape, my dorm room becomes my stage and my reflection in the mirror is my audience.

When the sadness sets in, I turn on the music and dance. A funny thing happens—a smile escapes my lips. And there is a specific reason for my smile…my father is watching me and laughing. Dancing in my bedroom at home, he would laugh and comment on how I made as much noise as an elephant dancing. He would have to turn up the volume of the television in the downstairs living room!

I know he's watching me from heaven, and he knows I dance just for him. I used to dance to forget—now I dance to remember. I remember him sitting in the audience at my recitals. I remember sitting on his lap after dinner, even at the old age of nineteen. I remember my mother telling me how proud he was of me and my dancing.

And I dance for another reason—I dance because I won't dance with him at my wedding.

So, know that dance is a wonderful thing. It has a healing power all its own. Talking and writing helps me work through my feelings, but dancing heals the pain and allows me to smile when nothing else has the power to make me.

Dancing is my way of talking to my father in heaven without uttering a single word.

I love you Dad.

Danielle Piccarini

Let Go

***Learning to dance gives you the greatest freedom of all: to express with your whole self the person you are.** ~Melissa Hayden*

Let go

Just let go

Your spirit will guide you

Let go of the anger

Let go of the hurt

Let go of the tears

Just let go

Flow with the rhythm

Feel the song

Hear your spirit

And let go...

And just be...

And dance.

Jennifer Coon

teammates

Ask not what your teammates can do for you.
Ask what you can do for your teammates." ~ Magic Johnson

Teammates

Teammates multiply the good in life and divide its evils.

Teammates should be Radical, Fanatical, and Most of

All, Mathematical!!

Teammates should be Radical;

They should love you when you're unlovable,

Hug you when you're unhuggable,

And bear you when you're unbearable.

Teammates should be Fanatical;

They should cheer when the whole world boos,

Dance when you get good news,

And cry when you cry too.

But most of all, teammates should be Mathematical,

They should multiply the joy, Divide the sorrow,

Subtract the past, And add to tomorrow,

Calculate the need deep in your heart,

And always be bigger than the sum of all their parts.

Author Unknown
Adapted by Sue Ann Kawecki for *Teammates*

Tanvi

Friends are as companions on a journey, who ought to aid each other to persevere in the road to a happier life. ~ **Pythagoras**

I don't exactly know what possessed me to try out for the dance team my freshman year of high school. I wasn't familiar with the team or the dancers on it. I was only aware of the general stereotype that goes along with being on pom-pom squads: the superficial, ditzy girls in short skirts shaking huge, brightly colored pieces of plastic on the football field.

I certainly did not look the part. Living through the punk music stage of my adolescent years, I was most definitely not the candidate for Miss School Spirit. None of my punker friends wanted anything to do with dance teams or school spirit. All I knew was that I loved to dance and wanted high school to be more than just the schoolwork. I didn't actually think I would ever make it, but hey, I did.

Once I made the team, I had no clue what to expect. The first day of practice I knew not a single soul. I recognized some of the girls that were in my grade, but I had never spoken more than twenty words to any of them in my entire life, and frankly I had never wanted to. So for half the year, I didn't utter a peep unless directly spoken to.

Everyone was nice to me, but I didn't feel at home. Little cliques had formed and I wasn't a part of any of them. I didn't mind for the time being-- I still had my own friends and a whole other life out of poms. Sometimes, though, I felt lost and out of place. If I hadn't loved performing and dancing so much I might have quit.

However, the first year progressed into my second and I began feeling more and more comfortable. My teammates became my friends, and I was happier going to practices. However, poms increasingly took up more of my time and I saw less and less of my old friends. Not being exactly close with any of my teammates yet, I got pretty lonely.

Going into my second season, my coach announced that any one-year veteran of the squad could try out for the next season's captain positions. Suddenly the three other juniors-to-be and I had something in common--extreme amounts of determination and stress! What an honor it would be to be the first junior captain ever! And how unbelievably scary tryouts were, seeing as all six candidates for captain seemed to be equally qualified for the job. The entire tryout situation, however, would soon bring us upperclassmen closer together.

I knew I had it in me to be a great captain, but I also realized that I had been mute my entire first year; and what kind of leader doesn't speak unless spoken to? The other five girls were much more assertive. I wanted to kick myself for thinking that people wouldn't like me if I talked and opened up to them. As the captain tryouts loomed nearer, I realized that I was to blame for not having any close friends on the squad because I hadn't given anyone the chance to get to know the real me.

On the day of the tryouts, tragedy struck one of my fellow teammates, Tanvi. She got horribly sick. Tryouts for captain were postponed. Then, right before the re-scheduled tryouts, Tanvi badly injured her knee. Captain announcements couldn't be delayed any longer, and Tanvi was named first Junior Captain, gimpy knee and all. We three other juniors naturally were annoyed, and although looking back now I can see that she was clearly the best one for the job, I, at the time, thought that the decision was extremely unfair.

Tanvi was in my lunch period that second year. I'm not exactly sure why she started talking to me more. I do know that I shielded my raging jealousy from her in my ongoing efforts to please other people. Maybe my silence was a grateful reprieve for her from the other two annoyed and more vocal juniors. Whatever the case, I was able to move past my grudge. I'm glad. She definitely needed a friend those first months she was captain, because we made a job that is difficult to begin with a 1000 times harder for her.

First of all, she was a junior, and her fellow juniors all felt that they should be in her place. So we were all quick to question her and we constantly thought that each one of us would be doing a better job. Secondly, having injured her knee, she couldn't actively participate for half the year. I think she felt like a dictator from the sidelines. How frustrating that must have been, telling us what to do without actually being able to do it herself! Finally, her two co- captains were seniors and best friends. Although they were all supposedly equals, more people naturally looked up to the older girls. When there were conflicting opinions and decisions that had to be made, the two best friends often sided against Tanvi. In the meanwhile, she and I had started hanging out more that year, and we shared classes together. So although I wasn't the greatest friend in the world, she soon felt close enough to me to share her feelings when the times got rough.

Tanvi was made of steel. Although her first year as captain was pretty rocky with them all constantly butting heads, we all survived, and she came out of it stronger than ever. Our senior year, we were best friends and co-captains. Tanvi was the experienced two-year captain, so yes, there were a few frustrations and jealousy issues, but we got through it and to this day, I admire her more than anyone in the world.

Tanvi worked so hard and always abided by the rules. She always stuck by her co-captains and by our coach. She wanted our squad to succeed so badly. She improved herself and all the girls, always emulating the ideal pom girl.

Being part of a team means working together toward a common goal. Am ideal teammate wants to perform her best for herself and more importantly, for her teammates. Tanvi was that teammate. She is the greatest friend, teammate, and captain I've ever had. Keeping her friendship in mind, every time we performed, I did it for myself, our squad, and especially for her.

Tanvi has backed me in everything I have done. Even though we are now out of high school and attending different universities, she still encourages me long-distance! I, to this day, have her on a high pedestal. No, she wasn't and isn't perfect; she has made her share of mistakes, but I guarantee that she never made the same mistake twice! Instead, she learns from it, and betters herself so it won't happen again. Her example made me a better captain, and her friendship has made me a better person.

Dance teams are about friends, spirit, and a passion that unites us all to work together. I was blessed to be a part of that, and doubly blessed to have discovered a best friend in Tanvi. My high school dance team days are over, but my teammates, especially my best friend, will be in my heart forever.

Katie Talkowsky

A Teammate's Survival Kit for Everyday Living

Spectacular achievement is always preceded by spectacular preparation.
~Robert H. Schuller

TOOTHPICK: reminds us to look for the good qualities in our teammates. You might be the only person who says something positive to them that day.

RUBBER BAND: reminds us that we need to be flexible. Things don't always go the way we plan, but flexibility will help it to work out.

BAND AID: reminds us that sometimes we do more than dance or cheer. That we help heal hurt feelings, broken dreams, and lend an ear to a teammate with a problem.

PENCIL: reminds us to be thankful and that we should count our blessings daily. We need to remind each other of our blessings and be proud of our accomplishments.

ERASER: reminds us that we are human, as are our teammates. Everyone makes mistakes, and it's okay. We must all be able to learn from our mistakes.

CHEWING GUM: reminds us to stick it out and to encourage each other to do likewise. Even the most impossible stunt or move can be accomplished by sticking to it.

MINT: reminds us that as a team and as individuals, we are all worth a mint. (Hey, maybe not everyone else thinks so, but we are!)

CANDY KISS: reminds us that everyone needs a hug or a kiss at least once a day. Even your coach!!

TEA BAG: reminds us that we need to take the time to relax. Not all our time needs to be spent learning or perfecting a routine. We need to take the time to enjoy each other.

A teammate must be willing to show their fellow teammates just how much she cares!

Author Unknown
Adaptation for Teammates by Sue Ann Kawecki

Best Friend

"Chance made us sisters; talent made us teammates; hearts made us friends."

Indeed, best friends are special people; but my best friend is extra special. Her name is Shaina and I have known her my entire life.

Ever since I can remember, I have looked up to her. To me, her thoughts were not opinions, they were simply the only ones that ever counted. When I was small, I loved to watch Mr. Rogers. That is, until this mature girl two years my elder informed me that all the cool people watched MTV. Well, then, there was no more of that Mr. Rogers! While she was at school, I watched MTV simply to win her approval. I eagerly wrote down the videos that I saw and the words that I heard although I was not old enough to understand the lyrics much less know what was going on! It didn't matter—I couldn't wait until she got home to show her how cool I was and then for us to resume our never-ending game of Barbies.

We spent numerous hours playing with those dolls. Most of time, I was busy changing their outfits so Shaina could give them her stamps of approval. Yet as everything must, all good things come to an end. The years went by, I joined her at the school and the Barbies just sat on a shelf collecting dust.

But an exciting chapter in both of our lives was just beginning. As a sixth grader, I wanted to try out for the middle school cheerleading squad. Shaina, in eighth grade, was already on the squad. She, being the cool eighth grader that she was, always found the time to help me, the pathetic sixth grader, out with everything--from my confidence to my high-V's. She was the best, and thanks to her, I made the squad.

Only now I was on my own, since Shaina was graduating and was going to high school. Again, my best friend was leaving me and would no longer be around to look out for me. In fact, Shaina switched from cheerleading to poms once she became a sophomore. But that was okay—I continued on my own as a cheerleader and was eventually the captain of my freshman squad.

As my freshman year came to a close, I came to a crossroad. Shaina would be a senior the following year and it would be the last year we would be together before she went off into the big world. Both the cheerleading and poms tryouts were just around the corner. If I joined poms, I would be given the opportunity to spend more time with Shaina before she left. I was so confused; how could I not be a cheerleader; yet, how could I let us spend our last year together, apart? So reluctantly I tried out and made the pom squad, with all intentions of returning to my beloved cheerleading the following year. But as the year progressed, I began to see what Shaina loved so much about poms.

As my love for poms increased, so did my love for Shaina. She was one of the captains of the squad and for the first time in my life I saw a side to her that hadn't been revealed to me until now. I saw how other people listened to her and respected her in a way that I always knew she deserved.

Shaina is a born leader and one day I hope I can carry on in her footsteps. I'd be happy being half the person that she is! And as I sit here writing this, this is the night of her very last senior game and I can't help but to feel sad. How am I going to get through my next few years on poms without her?

Shaina is not only my best friend, my teammate, my captain, my super hero, but she is also my sister. I don't know what I did to deserve such a great sister but I feel very fortunate to have her in my life. In a few months she will be going off to college, and I will have to start yet another chapter in my life. But no matter what, I will always have my memories—especially of our year together on poms.

I just hope that she realizes just how special she is to me. Even though we argue occasionally (hey we all do), I just want to tell her that no matter where she goes from here I will always cherish our times together and will always be here for her.

Allison Kaye

Destiny

No distance of place or lapse of time can lessen the friendship of those who are thoroughly persuaded of each other's worth. ~**Robert Southey**

Ruth Anne, Diann, and I were destined to become friends. Little did we know we would share this fated friendship for more than thirty years…

In the summer of 1969, before I left for college, my family took a trip. On our way from Iowa to Colorado we stopped in Cozad, Nebraska for a quick ice cream cone. A sweet girl waited on us. That very same evening we camped at a park in Julesburg, Colorado and were awakened by a bunch of noisy teenagers in cars.

A mere two weeks later the girl at the Dairy Queen (Diann), a girl with the noisy teenagers (Ruth Anne), and I would meet at Nebraska Christian College. Fate had brought us together and thus began our lifelong friendship.

As freshmen at this small Christian college, we were isolated. But soon enough, with much in common amongst the three of us, we found consolation in our growing friendship. Besides going steady with boys back home, we all liked to wear short skirts (which got us in constant trouble) and to shop at the mall (a reason for many a road trip).

A month into the school year a sign went up announcing cheerleader tryouts for the upcoming basketball season. It sounded like a blast, so the three of us signed up. We practiced and prayed. The day of tryouts arrived and we all did great! We were more than thrilled when we all made it.

Over the next few weeks we became even closer. For one thing there were the grueling practices. If we weren't practicing, we were busy sewing our own uniforms. (This was back in the day before ready-made uniforms). We made a great sewing team!

Sure we loved performing at the pep rallies and making the spirit posters that decorated the school. There was one problem however…although we enjoyed wearing the uniform, the skirt was a little long for our tastes! To alleviate the problem, we would roll up our skirts on game day. By doing so, our skirts were just as short as the skirts of our great friends, the junior college cheerleaders! [Smile]

We were happy but our dean was not. Time and time again, we were caught and together we suffered whatever punishment the dean meted. "Your skirt can only be two inches above the knee," our college handbook dictated. Our junior college counterparts, however, lived freely by the motto "Anything goes," and thrived during the era of the miniskirt.

Getting to the basketball games was quite a challenge as well. Everyone traveled to the games in cars instead of buses. One cold night a girl with an unreliable car agreed to drive the three of us. Of course, on the way, her engine blew up. We had to stand out and "thumb" a ride to the game. To get home (which took three hours) we had to squeeze in with the basketball players. I don't think they really minded all that much.

When the season was over our friendship was sealed…

The following year I returned to the college. Ruth Anne and Diann did not. They were both busy planning their weddings. I stayed on as a cheerleader and was elected captain of the squad. Although Ruth Anne and Diann were only my cheerleading teammates for a year, they have been my teammates through this game called life.

Cheerleading was such a positive experience! Today I am the cheerleading coach for middle schoolers. I still love it and I'm still cheering!

Mary Ahrenholtz

Recover

*No man fails who does his best... ~*Orison Swett Marden

The air sparked with tension as the girls stood huddled together in the Sundome's corridor. Nervously, they straightened their orange and black uniforms one last time, knowing that this was the moment they had worked eight long months for...

They had reached the American Open finals. For the first time ever, the squad was about to compete on a national level.   After placing third at a local invitational and first in their suburban regional, the Falcon girls were psyched for the American Open Nationals. After having performed a near-flawless routine in the preliminaries, they earned a spot in the finals.

The coordinator, signaling to them that they were "on deck", ushered the squad into a corner of the auditorium. Knowing that their performance was only moments away, they huddled around me. As I gave them a few final words of encouragement, seventeen glitter-covered faces stared back at me intently.

"You have all worked very hard to make it this far, and no matter what, I love you all. I am so proud of you. You have what it takes to win this! Just relax, smile and give it your all," I said, blowing kisses at all of them.

A high school squad from Florida was taking the mat as I walked over to the DJ station. Their routine looked clean, but one of their stunts fell. I looked over at my squad. They knew that the team's unfortunate bauble just might be their opening. If they could stick their routine, they just might have a shot at winning.

"And now, let's hear it for the Yankee girls, all the way from Fairless Hills, Pennsylvania...Pennsbury High School!" the emcee's voice boomed through the Sundome.

The girls bounded out onto the mat, bursting with enthusiasm and energy. They took their places as the music began. Their opening liberty sequence, always troublesome, was clean and solid. Their spirit showed; their expressions the best I'd ever seen. Entering the cheer portion of the routine, they executed amazing toe touches. It wasn't until the pyramid sequence at the end of the cheer that things went haywire...

The girls had been performing their heel stretch pyramid perfectly now for months. Today, however, I watched it go up and come crashing down. I couldn't understand what had happened, all I could think was, Come on girls, recover, RECOVER!

As they set up for the last segment of their routine, I held my breath. I still couldn't understand why the pyramid had fallen...it never fell. Toe touch basket tosses loaded up as the remaining girls performed toe touches on the ground. It looked good, except that Julie, one of the sophomores, had only gotten about six inches off the ground in her touch. Julie's jumps were excellent, so for the second time that day, I was baffled.

I watched as the girls moved into the next dance formation, keeping my eye on Julie. Usually a great dancer, Julie's motions were good but her smile looked forced and fake, and she was limping as she moved. As the squad moved into their ending stunt, my worst fears were confirmed. Julie had been injured. Julie, an experienced flyer, only had to perform an elevator prep, and rotate it forward. Her bases made a valiant attempt to get her up into the stunt by lifting her from the ground, as she clung to their heads with her knees bent. As hard as they tried the bases just couldn't lift her, and the stunt tumbled to the ground, almost taking the stunt next to it down as well.

The girls continued to cheer to the crowd, many of them not realizing what had happened. I bolted toward the mat. Julie collapsed onto me, tears careening down her cheeks.

"My knee, my knee, something's wrong," she squeaked between sobs. In a split second, her sixteen teammates encircled her, wondering what had happened. Apparently, when she performed her front hurdler during the cheer, her knee had snapped. By the time the routine was over, Julie couldn't walk.

The trainer bent over Julie's knee, as she cried and cried. Her best friend, Michelle, held her hand tightly. The trainer believed she had torn her ACL, a major ligament in the knee. This only made Julie cry harder.

The rest of the girls gathered around the monitor to watch a replay of their performance. As they watched, tears streamed down their every cheek. The captains, clinging to each other in supportive hugs, sobbed uncontrollably. Stunned, all the girls sadly thought about how close they had been. Remorsefully, they watched the last squad in their division execute a solid routine with only a few minor wobbles.

Julie's pain-filled cries, were drowned out by her litany of apologies, "I'm sorry, I'm sorry, I'm so sorry."

As I watched the tape, my jaw dropped and tears began to run down my very own cheeks. But my tears fell for a different reason. As I watched Julie struggle through the routine, I felt her pain. She had hurt herself a mere twenty seconds into the routine. For the next two minutes, Julie had endured the pain, and even had attempted to jump, all for the sake of the squad. She knew if she walked off the mat, they had no chance of winning at all. She truly had given that routine everything she had had in her.

Later that evening, after making a trip to the hospital, Julie returned to our hotel. She returned to the hotel with her leg immobilized by a brace. After being showered with kisses and hugs from her teammates, she informed us that the doctor had pretty much determined that yes, she had torn her ACL, and would need surgery to repair it.

The lost competition was forgotten. The girls were merely happy to have come thus far and more importantly, were thankful that Julie would be okay. The girls helped Julie take her bath in her bathing suit so she could get ready for dinner.

Now, whenever we need to give something our all, I remind the team of Julie and how she had recovered to give us everything that she had.

Deana Ellison

Trust

The glory of friendship...the spiritual inspiration that comes when he discovers that someone else believes in him and is willing to trust him.
~Ralph Waldo Emerson

There is always somewhere you can go

To let your thoughts and feelings flow

Out of your heart and out of your mind

Then you feel as if there is some kind

Of connection that makes you feel serene

Or a shoulder upon which you know you could lean

When you feel the pressure of life's test

Knowing in you it brings out your best

Judgment and choices you could make on your own

But the feelings and decisions weren't felt alone

For you talked and talked for a long long while

You walked in with a frown and out with a smile

About something you thought would be so hard

When all you had to do was let down your guard

And explain your feelings to that person you trust

Who helps you when you need to adjust

And release from the burden that you so bear

That is easy to carry if only you'd share

The load with someone you feel close to

And together you can find the right answer to

The question that had put you on your quest

When suddenly you realize you have passed your test

That you know you could not have done alone

If you hadn't reached out to someone you've known

You've reached the serenity in life you lust

When you simply relied on your friend whom you trust.

Jeremy Cramm

Her Spirit Lives On

*Never shall I forget the days I spent with you…~*Ludwig Van Beethoven

It was Saturday, October 18, 1997. I awoke to brilliant sunshine and unseasonably warm temperatures, and could sense that this would be a day like no other. The anticipation of the day and the memories that would forever be etched in my soul overwhelmed me. Soon I would join thirteen members of my former alma mater cheerleading squad in what would be the experience of a lifetime. PURDUE HOMECOMING '97.

The Athletic Public Relations staff had invited all former university cheerleaders to return to the campus for the Homecoming weekend festivities. Many activities had been planned for the weekend, but the main event would be taking the field during Saturday's game and cheering the Boilermakers team on to victory. This would be a golden opportunity for alumni to reunite and once again experience the excitement of Big Ten football from the field. It would be an opportunity to show that the cheerleading spirit within us lives on…generation after generation.

Having been a member of the Purdue cheerleading squad in the mid '70s, I felt fortunate to belong to such an elite group of individuals. We had experienced various trials and tribulations, victories and defeats; but through it all, one element exceeded all others. The friendships that were born and nurtured through countless hours of travel, practice and games would be the one entity that would reunite us.

Although twenty years and many miles had come between us, we still shared a common bond. We had a spirit in us to rekindle these friendships, to pull together and to once again become one. Having not seen many of these former "teammates" since graduation, we decided to start our reunion at a predetermined location the night before the big game. After all, we had twenty years of catching up to do. Everyone was inspired to bring pictures and other memorabilia so as to reminisce of days gone by.

As the time grew nearer, emotions ran high for everyone. There was the thrill of seeing faces that had over the years, become only memories. We were all anxious to meet one another's families, to follow career paths and to rejuvenate our friendships. But in the midst of all this excitement, there was also a heartbreaking reality we were wishing didn't exist. We all felt emptiness in our hearts because a member of our cheerleading family would not be joining us.

We had lost a dear friend and teammate in an automobile accident a few months prior to this reunion. It was an unbelievable shock to each and every one of us; and it left us with so many unanswered questions. How could someone so kind and giving be gone without us having the opportunity to thank her for being our friend? From the hugs we received and the tears that we shed, we came to realize that this "family" reunion would be the beginning of our healing process.

At this small gathering, were the husband, the 7 year-old daughter and the 4 year-old son of our beloved friend. Having only met a couple of squad members prior to this weekend, this family had taken it upon themselves to travel many miles to join us and to help fill the emptiness of our hearts. It was the best thing that could have happened to us. It was nice to know that a part of our friend was indeed with us that night and would continue to be with us forever.

As the events of the Homecoming celebration unfolded on Saturday, the excitement of the day could be felt and seen in every direction. Once again donning a cheerleading outfit and running down the field amidst a sell-out crowd was a dream come true. With the band playing and banners waving, the 70+ alumni cheerleaders took the field. Among our ranks was the daughter of our teammate Paula. Dressed in matching uniform and wearing the smile of a true cheerleader, she stole the hearts of the crowd. She was quite comfortable in these surroundings…almost as if she had been here before.

As the "All American" Marching Band played "Hail Purdue", a chill ran up my spine. It was the same sensation I had experienced each and every time I had ever heard the song over the past twenty years. As for the tear in my eye, it existed for two reasons…one for the emptiness in my heart for my friend, the other for the smile on her little girl's face—giving me peace within—knowing that <u>Her spirit lives on</u>.

In memory of Paula Richert Loving

Purdue University Cheerleader

1975-1978

Jane Yundt

The Back Row Club

There's nothing worth the wear of winning but laughter, and the love of friends. ~Hilaire Beloc

It all started as a way to keep busy. My freshman year cheerleading season had come to an end. With encouragement from my friends, I tried out for the school dance team. One of my friends Kristin and I soon found ourselves as the newest additions to the team. Although we were ecstatic to have made it, we knew that we were way behind the older and more experienced members of the team. Sure, we had both taken dance lessons in the past, but our training could not hold a candle to that of the other girls.

While we got along with our teammates on the sidelines, Kristin and I could not help but to feel inferior to them on the dance floor. For every routine, there seemed to be spots reserved in the back row with our names engraved on them! It even got to the point where we would automatically walk to the back row as soon as our captains announced a formation change. It became a constant joke for us. We named ourselves the two honorary members of the "Back Row Club".

At summer camp, Kristin and I roomed together. By this time, we were used to being the worst dancers on the squad. We learned to laugh at ourselves, rather than to cry, whenever we messed up. Although we struggled in the lower level classes, we always were there to cheer on our captains as they perfected their elite level dances.

We held tremendous respect for our captains and their dance abilities. One day we hoped to be like them. The respect was reciprocated. They often commented on our good attitudes and dedication.

Kristin and I were finally given the chance to get out of the back row during the football season. The school band had added two more numbers to their halftime show. While the majority of the squad performed to the "River Dance", Kristin, another girl and I were placed in the "Giesha Girls" dance. Supposedly, "River Dance" was reserved for the old members. We watched in awe as the old members performed with their flying brightly-colored scarves. We were so jealous because we knew that our dance would be terrible.

Not only was it terrible, but also the third girl had quit the team, leaving Kristin and me to dance alone on the field! To convince the crowd that we were truly geisha girls, we wore the most hideous masks and had to wave around ugly brown fans. It was beyond embarrassing…

The first time that we performed the routine at a football game Kristin and I could not stop ourselves from laughing from behind the masks. We weren't the only ones laughing though. I vividly remember the crowd's laughter, the giggles of our teammates and the humored looks on the band members' faces. I sincerely hoped that they were laughing with us rather than at us; but looking back now, I really don't think that that was the case! The only person whom I didn't see laughing was the band director. It struck him as so "unfunny" that he threatened to kick Kristin and me off the field if we didn't get serious.

Competition season soon rolled around and either all of our hard work paid off or our captains simply felt sorry for us. Miraculously, Kristin and I found ourselves in the front row of our jazz dance. Our sense of accomplishment was not dimmed by the fact that we had the spotlight for all of two eight-counts! We had reached our goal—we were not ALWAYS relegated to the back row. We ended up placing first in state with that dance and Kristin and I jokingly decided that it was all because of our fifteen seconds of fame.

The end of our season was greeted by tears. I learned that I had to move 600 miles to a new state. I was being forced to leave behind my friends, my school, and the dance team. During my one year on that dance team I had discovered so much about myself--my love for dance, the realization that I could accomplish anything if I applied myself, and most importantly, the true friendship and camaraderie that I shared with Kristin.

At my new school, I continued to dance and as a senior, I was one of the squad's captains. From the other side of the mirror, I saw the new girls on the team and I empathized with their struggles. I knew how it felt to always be a prominent member of the "Back Row Club".

It was ironic— I encouraged the new girls to keep practicing; I knew how they felt— I used to be in their shoes and yet they looked at me with eyes that seemed to say,

"Uh huh—sure you were!" How could have I, their captain, who was front and center in all the dances possibly have known that feeling of inferiority?

I don't expect anyone to accept my success story until they live one of their own. Until then, I encourage everyone to realize their potential and discover that passion for dance. I just hope they all have their own Kristins to help and see them through it.

Shaina Kaye

Daily Therapy

"When life begins to shed a tear, just perk up and say a cheer."

Every little girl dreams of one day becoming a cheerleader. It's not that they want to have awesome toe touches, to overcome their fears of heights by doing liberty fulls, or to spread school spirit at games. None of that matters to most little girls. Simply, the portrayal of cheerleaders as gorgeous and popular is quite appealing.

Growing up, I too dreamed of being a cheerleader. Watching "Saved By the Bell" and reading "Sweet Valley Twins" books strengthened my belief that all cheerleaders were popular and had cute football-playing boyfriends. With that ideal in mind, I found no other sport as interesting.

By the time I started high school, I was looking to get seriously involved in an activity or sport. I had heard about the cheerleading tryouts, but I had never stopped to think that it might actually be more than just a pipedream. I had never taken dance or gymnastic classes. The only experience I had had with "spirit" was a brief one-year stint on the grade school pep club. Despite my life-long dream, I initially discarded the idea of even trying out.

But the more I thought about it, the more attractive the whole idea was. A couple of my friends were going to do it and they convinced me that I did have the potential and ability to make it. So, seizing the day, I signed up. Trying out turned out to be the most fun and at the same time, the scariest, thing I did my freshman year. Scary as it was, I made it.

In less than a month, my new teammates and I had learned the seventy-something cheers, had practiced jumps, and had started building. But the fact of the matter was, we were still not a very talented squad. To us, being able to cradle from a half was something to be proud of! Some could do a full, but for the most part, our builds were very juvenile.

We unfortunately had a lot of inter-squad squabbles. People talked behind one another's backs and made minimal attempts to hide it. That made my first year of cheering even that much harder. Many people, who had once shared my cheerleading ideal, ended up quitting. I definitely wanted to as well, but I stuck with it.

Football and basketball seasons came and went and tryouts were just around the corner. I was terrified of once again being on the squad. But like the previous year, a bunch of my friends were trying out. I hoped that with friends in my corner, I might have an easier time of dealing with the veteran cheer members.

That summer, we attended camp. We had never worked harder. We learned cheers, chants and dances quicker than we ever had before. We were sore, tired and a little discouraged. Having never been to camp, we felt inferior to the other teams. But, ironically, our inferiority complex helped us to come together.

The camp experience gave us a taste of what true cheerleading was all about. The rest of the summer we strived to become a better squad. We improved our half-time shows, yelled louder, made our motions sharper, and practiced our tumbling and jumps. More importantly, we got along better. If someone on the team had a problem with someone else, they worked hard to resolve it. Practices went from something I dreaded to something I greatly looked forward to.

We started the new school year with a newfound confidence. And it showed. Compliments about our improvement flooded in. We didn't let it go to our heads though; we knew that we still had a long way to go and we were willing to work to get there.

Mid-football season I started to notice something—whenever I got depressed, upset or angry, all I had to do was to go to practice to feel better. Surrounded by the people who had become my closest friends, I managed to deal with my problems through cheerleading. Cheerleading had become my daily dose of therapy.

Awhile back, I went through a particularly hard time. I had reached a point where I felt isolated. No one seemed to understand me. One day, it got so bad, in fact, that I harbored some pretty serious thoughts about suicide. "Okay," I thought to myself, "I just need to make it until the end of practice." All I could think about was that bottle of ibuprofen in the medicine cabinet and whether I could actually go through with it.

But halfway through practice, I reluctantly laughed along with my teammates. By the end of practice, we were rolling on the ground. The shared laughter broke through my self-imposed shell and gave me a little hope that yes, things can get better!

As cheerleaders, we go through a lot together. We are often stereotyped as being snobs, idiots, and a few not-so-nice names. To get through it, we have to rely on each other and have faith. Together as a team we can overcome and become the best we can be. The important thing is to not take the experience for granted. It's a way to relax, to let go, to laugh, and to share with friends. It's that and so much more...it's my daily therapy session.

Michelle Rutherfurd

Teamwork=Victory

Alone we can do so little; together we can do so much. ~Helen Keller

Life without cheerleaders is a life without excitement. Imagine how dull a football or basketball game would be without a group of smiling faces there, whose sole purpose is to encourage and uplift. The game would be missing its soul! Cheerleaders play an enormous role in bursting that inner bubble of spirit residing in the depths of each fan. Together, cheerleaders and the fans interact with the team to give them that needed drive to win. If you take a minute to think about why some sports teams are consistently victorious, and why cheer squads are so effective in creating an unforgettable sporting event, you'll see that it always comes down to teamwork!

Teamwork made my high school cheerleading experiences worthwhile. I was a proud participant of our school's inaugural team. We brought cheerleading alive. Establishing a new program went hand in hand with building trusting relationships amongst the new squad's teammates.

Twelve fantastic girls made up this fresh squad. We didn't initially start out as friends, much less teammates. However, we soon overcame this first hurdle. Our coach, Brenda was a big fan of team bonding. During the summer, she allotted a portion of each practice to activities such as the human knot or group scavenger hunts. We spent many an afternoon in teammate Bethany's pool. Parades, community work, car washes, and garage sales gave us the time to strengthen our bonds. Being a close-knit squad gave new meaning and greater pride in being a Crimson cheerleader!

Those summer cheer practices gave us only a taste of true teamwork. It was not until we attended UCA summer camp that we realized how important we had to be to each other to succeed. Being the new squad of cheerleaders amongst many other veteran teams and experienced cheerleaders was scary, intimidating, and exciting all at the same time. However, being exposed to it gave us the motivation to give us 110%. If our stunts, our motions, and our dance abilities lacked perfection, our spirit as a squad could not be topped! Shining through, our spirit got us noticed.

On the final day of camp, 'All Stars', 'Superior Squad', and 'Most Improved Squad', and 'UCA Leadership' awards were presented. The staff members informed us earlier that the most prestigious award was the 'UCA Leadership Award'. We didn't have high expectations for being awarded that one. After all, we were a new squad. If anything, I expected us to receive the 'Most Improved" award. Within a span of four days, we had improved from executing a side thigh stand to a step-in elevator!

"And the 1997 'UCA Leadership Award' goes to …the Maple Grove Crimson!" proclaimed our head camp instructor. Although our skill was not the best, our attitude and enthusiasm made us stand out amongst the rest. As we graciously accepted the award, we were riding high on emotions of pride and happiness. We proudly placed the trophy in our school's trophy case—not only our very first contribution to the case, but the first trophy ever in the new school's history.

Being a part of that cheer squad, I experienced the time of my life. The teamwork brought out the spirit in me. The next time you step foot onto the sidelines or onto the practice gym floor, remember this: even when you've cheered the game of your life, it's not the step-in elevator you'll remember. In time, you'll forget the cheers, the stunts and the faces in the crowd, but you will never forget your teammates!!

Lindsey Nodgaard

Making It Worth It

Coming together is a beginning, staying together is progress, and working together is success. ~Henry Ford

'Give your all' was our motto,

'But if we fail today,

Hey-we still have tomorrow!'

But now when I wake from a night's sleep,

Poms is nothing more than a dream…

From tryouts to routine auditions,

Car washes and our competitions,

Doubles, foettes, and high kicks,

Switch leaps, illusions, and of course our splits.

What was yesterday's #1 priority

Is only today's lasting memory.

Remember that old radio that barely had sound?

But nevertheless lifted us off the ground?

Formations, changes, and always more questions,

Who'd ever thought we'd take more than second?

But the smiles on our faces reflected what we knew—

That if we tried our very best…Oh, the things we could do!

For three years long, we practiced hard to make perfect.

But in the end it was the teammates, not the victories that made it worth it!

Nikisha McDonald

success

Success is not the result of spontaneous combustion. You must set yourself on fire."

I Made It!

There are no secrets to success. It is the result of preparation, hard work, learning from failure. ~General Colin L. Powell

Can I make the cheerleading team?

It seems so out of reach.

All the girls are so talented,

And I'm so hard to teach.

Will the coach there like me?

What about the rest?

Win or lose, I'll give my all,

and know I did my best.

I so want to be a cheerleader,

It's always been my dream.

Being part of the pep rallies,

And rooting on the team.

Yesterday the list was posted.

My name amongst the few.

A moment of silence before I screamed,

I made it, I've done it,

Thank God that it's through!

Melissa Prussing

Give It Your All

"Dance every performance as if it were your last."

The gym has hushed to an eerie silence
A thousand eyes stare down upon me
Prodding with their timeless stare
Motivating me to succeed

I return their gaze with confidence
As the music I know so well begins
I know I'm performing my very best.
I don't want this feeling to ever end.

Now it's done and over
Another girl begins her routine.
I've endured months of practice and perseverance
For two minutes of fame.

It's later now; the judging is complete.
Soon they will call first place.
Whatever I end up with, I will be proud
Because I know in my heart, I gave it my all today.

Courtney Andreone

Pazzazz Prayer

...(P)rayer is a support for all other efforts. ~George Buttrick

Now I lay me
Down to sleep,
Tomorrow I'll dance,
I'll spin and leap.

Bless my legs
And bless my feet,
Help them both
To hit the beats.

Bless my arms
So that judges will see,
That they're as sharp
As sharp can be.

Bless my face
With expressions so great.
Attitude or smiles,
Make them all first-rate.

Bless my body with energy
And lots of spunk
So that I can keep up
With all that funk.

Bless the other teams
As they take the floor,
But let the judges like us

Just a little bit more.

Bless our family and our friends
Who support us throughout the year,
No matter how we perform
They're always ready to cheer.

Bless the Pazzazz
On our way to state,
And help us to accept
Whatever our fate.

We've all practiced hard
Now bless us with rest,
So that tomorrow our team
Can do its very best.

Amen.

Doneeta Kallal

First Place

Only those that dare to fail greatly can ever achieve greatly.
~Robert F. Kennedy

The heat from the lights that surrounded us had gone unnoticed. The cameras that followed our every movement had ceased to exist. The people in the stadium had swiftly changed into tiny blurs of the human form, hardly recognizable, and I was certain that their numbers had multiplied.

Out on that floor, that allotted space for us to contain our routine, we had attempted to perform the way we knew we could. We had hoped, toiled and worked towards this goal for so many months. The "here and now" had been our only chance to make our dreams a reality.

Our performance was less than perfect. So misplaced among our many successful routines that it seemed unreal ... more like a cruel joke than anything else. The preliminary round of the competition was over and done, and with it disappeared our only chance for a national title. Before I had left for the NCA All Star Cheerleading Nationals in Dallas, Texas, my sights had been set on sweeping the championship. Those sights had been quickly replaced with a desperate wish to merely make the final rounds. All of our hard work just had to pay off in some form! How could we possibly return home, after placing fifth in the nation the previous year, with nothing to now show for our efforts? I couldn't imagine venturing back into the arena the next day as a spectator.

As I sat, keeping track of each team's score in my program, questions raced through my mind. How could we have performed so poorly? What went wrong out there? Will there be any chance for us to make the top fifteen and qualify for finals? It was then, as the teams continued to perform and push us even farther down in the standings, that I began to prepare myself for the inevitable heartache that I was all but certain would come.

On the other hand, I concluded that all had certainly not been lost. After all, we had achieved the honor of actually qualifying. We had been blessed with the opportunities to travel and to experience every little event that built up to this moment in time. We may not have reached the heights that we knew we were capable of reaching, but perhaps this served merely as a milestone in the path of experience—a lesson into the realization and comprehension of defeat.

Time passed. The impending moment of truth had finally arrived. Miraculously, the announcer informed us that we indeed had made Finals! We had just barely hung on to fifteenth place! This was clearly the opportunity of a lifetime, the answer to my prayers! We were being given a second chance—the chance to prove to ourselves, as well as to everyone else, that we would not accept failure without a fight.

The team pulled together like never before. We were intensely drawn together by the power of the situation. That following morning, when we went out onto that floor, we were determined to have the time of our lives. We were going to prove to everyone in that stadium that our performance of the previous afternoon had been nothing more than a fluke.

As we walked out once again onto that floor, I felt as though the entire auditorium was silently rooting for us, hoping that the humiliation of the previous day would not come back to haunt us. Now, looking back on those two and a half minutes under the spotlights, all is an unmemorable blur, but then the feeling I had as I came off of that floor is one that I won't ever forget. We had indeed performed the routine of our lives and we were on top of the world! That performance still reigns as one of my most treasured experiences.

The opportunity I had to participate in such an event remains unreal to me. Moving from fifteenth to seventh place in the nation is quite an accomplishment. Yet, even more than the placing and the hype that went with it, what mattered more was what I had learned. I learned what it's like to accept defeat, to truly rise to the occasion, and to be a part of something bigger than myself.

Some situations have the unbelievable power to pull people together to create one cohesive unit—this was one of them. Maybe you don't really need the trophy after all to truly win first place.

Carly Colao

It Keeps Me Going

It's not knowing what you do, but doing what you know. **~Anthony Robbins**

Four years…35 football games, four competitions, six basketball half-times, 15 pep rallies, one trip, eight parades, six summer camps, 1000's of practice hours, and countless tears… That's how long I have been on the Tigerettes Drill Team.

I may not be the prettiest, thinnest, smartest, kindest or the most graceful dancer. But the things I have learned over the years have done much to inspire me to succeed. I would like to share the knowledge that keeps me going…

- Be kind. It comes back to you when you least expect it.

- Appreciate the little people. They aren't so 'little' when you need them for something.

- Take advantage of every opportunity to help another. Who knows when you will need assistance. Perhaps that person you helped will be there for you.

- Perfection is always just one step away. Never stop trying to reach for it; someday you just might get a taste of it, if only for a second.

- Always dance like it's your first performance. Remember how good that first applause felt?

- Know your strengths well, but know your weaknesses better.

- Don't let a bad day affect you. When you focus on the bad things, you tend to ignore all the good things that happen.

- Always remember the practices. Without the practices, performances mean nothing.

- Appreciate your parents. They love you more than anyone else you will ever meet.

- Go straight to the source of any problem. Griping does nothing but make the situation worse.

- Laugh.

- Smile. It's contagious.

- Say 'thank you'. Saying it is alarmingly simple, yet has great results.

- Mean it when you do.

- Don't be afraid to cry. Crying doesn't hurt anyone and it makes you feel better.

- Never ask to be the exception. You are not too weak to go by the rules.

- Sometimes it's better to do things for personal gratification, rather than for public recognition.

- Your audience most likely doesn't know the difference between a single and a triple… do what you can do the best you can do it and be proud.

- Dreams are only worthy if you honestly believe you can realize them.

- Sometimes it's better to be the hardest worker or the most eager one, rather than the one with the most natural talent.

The above might not serve as your own personal inspiration. And that's okay. We all have our own; it's merely a matter of discovering it.

Heather Reneau

Reach for the Stars

"Reach…

reach…

reach… for the stars!"

"This is it. I'm so nervous," I cried out. The announcer instructed all of us anxious cheerleaders to form our team circles on the mat. The gymnasium seemed enormous. The bleachers teemed with fans, wall to wall, and the floor buzzed with excited cheerleaders. Our terrified squad hurriedly sat down on the mat and we held hands as we anticipated the results. This was it…STATE…we had worked so hard the whole year for this day, for this moment. We tightened our grips as the announcer announced the tenth place team.

"A bright, starry future is ours!"

We had no clue where we had placed; there were twenty teams competing and only the top ten scorers were to be awarded. We knew that we were capable of winning, yet our performance had been sadly far from perfect. Things definitely hadn't gone right that day, and we were disappointed.

"No, please no," each of my teammates cried out as the places moved up, closer to first. We desired to be state champions more than anything; it was our ultimate goal. After the fourth place team was announced, my stomach churned, and my face paled. I closed my eyes and squeezed my teammates' cold yet sweaty hands. Memories of all the hard work, stress, and friendships I had shared with my teammates over the year flashed before me…

"Tighten up," Mrs. Walter's voice resonated in my ears as we repeatedly performed our cheer at practice. "You have to believe that you are state champions," she instructed. "Close your eyes and imagine yourself at State. Imagine everything happening the way you want things to be," our coach repeatedly told us.

She believed in us; we just had to believe in ourselves. We deserved this more than anyone. We had worked so hard for years. This was our chance to prove to everyone that our team was certainly capable of realizing its dreams...

Opening my eyes, I struggled to see through my tears. Through my blurred vision, I stared into the sea of impatient faces in the crowd.

"Look at Kelly," Rachel teased. "She looks like she's gonna puke." Kelly managed to smile nauseously back at us. We were all just as terrified of the results--we had either placed in the top three or we hadn't placed at all.

Then, the third place team was announced. It wasn't us! I didn't know what to think. I looked around at my teammates' faces as they all paled. I knew that we were all sharing the same feelings and at that moment I realized how close we truly were.

I closed my eyes and squeezed my teammates' hands tightly. I could hear Sasha's loud cries of "No, no, no," as the rest attempted to silence her in order to hear the announcer's voice.

"Starlight, Starbright,
wish we may, wish we might..."

"And now, second place goes to the team from..." the announcer paused for what seemed like hours, "Dewitt!" he finished.

"Oh my God," I gurgled as I began to cry.

"This is it!" my eager teammates cried out in disbelief. We were ecstatic, apprehensive and terrified all at once.

"Starlight, Starbright,
always keeping our goal in sight..."

"Please," I cried out to no one in particular. My hands trembled and I could barely breathe.

"And now, the 1999 Class B State Champion is the team from," the voice paused, "LLLLLL-inden," The words boomed over the speakers and rang in my ears. We sprang up immediately, releasing the tension and anxiety that had built up in each one of us.

Rachel and I hugged and cried as we ran up to accept the enormous trophy. "First place!" I screamed. "Can you believe this is really happening? We did it, first place!" I cried as I held the trophy high above my head, proudly displaying it for all to see.

Our fans rushed onto the mat to congratulate us as we all hugged and shared tears of pure joy and disbelief.

"We reached...reached...

reached... for the stars."

That day remains as one of the best days of my life. I will never forget that moment nor the feelings of unadulterated joy and victory for as long as I live. Earning the State championship taught me that as long as I believe, nothing is ever out of my reach.

"First place in the state, is finally ours!"

Haley Hanna

#1

"We don't have an attitude...we're just that good."

Only moments to go

We're waiting on the side.

For all we know

This could be our final ride.

Our stomachs are weak

And our bodies are sweating.

This will be our peak

There will be no forgetting.

The roar of the crowd

Is more than exciting.

But it doesn't stop the fear

That we all have been fighting.

The fear of failure--

It's a reality upon us.

But failure is impossible

If we keep our team promise.

The promise to give

Our absolute best--

That is the least we have to do

To beat the rest.

So we'll step on the floor

No more can be done.

The only thing left

Is to be number one.

Jeane DeRosa

Taking Chances

What isn't tried won't work. ~Claude McDonald

During my senior year, our co-ed squad traveled to Disney World to defend our national title and to hopefully make a "three-peat" as Americheer champions. Before we left for Florida, our coach called a meeting and made us a proposition.

"While we're in Florida, how would you like to compete in the US Spirit Nationals? It's held at Universal Studios the day after Americheer's. I think we should do it, " he said. However, "no" was the team's general consensus.

Dennis piped in, "I don't know about you guys, but I don't want to be stressed out on my vacation more than I absolutely have to be." His sentiment was shared by everyone.

Members from most competing teams will tell you that until you're off that blue mat, you experience frequent tummy butterflies and feelings of restlessness. Competing twice would double the anxiety that we already felt! Bottom line was simply that everyone would be thrilled to win two different national titles, but no one was willing to take the chance of losing and possibly tarnishing our standing record as champions. We had worked too hard for that...

~   ~

Drenched in a salty aura of sweat and tears, we returned to the resort after our victory celebration. We had just cheered with all our little Bison heart and had paraded away with a 3-peat championship title from Americheer! At this point, more than half the squad was content with winning just one championship. But in the end, Coach Siegal managed to coax us into chancing US Spirit the very next day. So the next morning we found ourselves reluctantly boarding the bus for Universal Studios.

During our warm up in a Universal Studios warehouse, I realized that perhaps entering in this competition wasn't all that it was cracked up to be. We were sore, overstretched and outright exhausted from the day before. Our most elementary stunts weren't hitting as flawlessly as usual. To top it off, the air was unbearably thick with the sneering scrutiny from the other co-ed teams in our division. A large blonde guy from an all-star team even snickered loudly at our toe touches and pike basket-tosses! (In Florida, back rotation in baskets is legal; however, in Illinois, it is not.) We quickly realized that to compete on the same caliber as the other squads, we had to throw together some quick back-tuck baskets. Needless to say, it was just too much. I think we were more nervous warming up in front of these other teams than we ever were performing on the mat in front of a crowd!

When we finally got on the floor, everything went surprisingly well—our walking opening mount went up smooth as butter, the tumbling hit, and we were as sharp as we've ever been known to be! As our first back-tuck basket went up, however, I spied a white-haired grandmother's pink-smattered lips open and drop as a large "Ohh!!" emitted from the crowd.

"Oh no, " I thought to myself. "They biffed! I knew that that basket was a dumb idea. Well—gotta sell the rest of the routine if we want to save face at all!"

After the performance, we ran off the mat and met behind the set. Coach said, "I'm very proud of you guys. You did the best that you could."

His pep talk was not making us feel any better about our chances of winning, however. The only thought that ran through my head was, "We should never have come here. What are we going to tell everyone when we get back home?"

Just as they began announcing the places, our squad formed a misshapen circle on the mats and held hands—sweaty palm to sweaty palm--ten percent humidity and ninety percent nerves. We squeezed tightly and shut our eyes as they started with the tenth place winners…

Nope. Not us. We looked up at each other for a quick smile and clenched our hands tighter. Nope, we weren't ninth place either. Wow, maybe that basket toss wasn't so bad after all! Then they announced fifth place and one of the most amazing squads was called. Teary-eyed at their "failure", they accepted the gorgeous golden trophy.

At that point, our circle dismembered as grips relaxed. As second place rolled around and was announced, we laughed at each other.

"Guys…we didn't even place!" Dennis laughed, shrugging his shoulders, synchronized with the arching of his black eyebrows.

It was obvious that we didn't really even care anymore. We had won our one championship and Siegal had said that this was "Just for fun", though I love to laugh at that comment, looking back at any competition! We never expected to win this one, but I was feeling a little disappointed that we hadn't even placed in the top ten.

Already having accepted failure, we started to discuss where we would meet for the bus. Amidst our chatter, I heard the announcer say...

"Our Champions...Buffalo Grove High School!"

Jenny got up and jumped on Tommy. But the rest of us were too shocked by this turn of events to even move. We just sent empty stares at each other from across the circle.

Leo whispered, "What?" That moment of disbelief seemed to last for five minutes, although it was merely seconds until Siegal yelled.

"You did it! I knew that you could!"

At that moment, our shock dissolved and everyone hopped up, screaming, and piling on top of one another. Carla grabbed me and we cried together. Looking over her shoulder, I glanced out at the Blue and Orange crowd of our families and fans. They were just as surprised and ecstatic as we were, waving their little "Bison" banners and shaking their rice noisemakers—just like they always do, whether we bring home a trophy or not.

That night we ran back to the resort and threw our coaches in the pool, as well as anyone else who got too close to the edge. I sat back on a lawn chair and looked on at my shrieking teammates, high from the victory, and thought, "This would never have been made possible if we hadn't taken the chance."

Alisa J. Monnier

Baby I'm A Star

Dancing is part of the soul; it feeds from the nourishment of the heart.
~Vladimar Lympthmon

There I sat, outside of the gym, my old, worn-out black leotard itching the very heart of me. I was nervously waiting for my turn to enter the gym for what seemed to be the most crucial moment of my life. Soon I would either be a member of my high school's dance team, the Tapaires, or a returning dancer on the junior varsity team.

My mind flashes back to that same day, one year earlier, when I had tried out for the team as well... I had finally been old enough to try out and I was ecstatic about the possibility of actually making the team. I had been dancing for as long as I could remember, and watching the Tapaires had been a favorite pastime. I had always dreamed of the day that I would make the team, and I had hoped that I wouldn't have to dream much longer.

I had thought I had a substantial chance of making it. The girls that had tried out with me hadn't done too well, so somewhere in the back of my mind I had thought that that might help me look better in the judges' eyes.

After everyone had tried out, the waiting game began. After what seemed like an eternity, we were asked to sit in a circle while the coach passed out the scores. Thirty nervous girls sat, papers turned upside down, waiting for the signal to flip our fates over. My thoughts kept contradicting one another. One minute I had total self-confidence; the next hopelessness reigned. These thoughts rushed through my mind about a million times until the coach finally told us to unveil our fates.

I had hesitated before looking at my flipped sheet. In that moment I saw some of the other girls' reactions. Some couldn't stop screaming, while others just sat there and sobbed. The girl next to me has asked me if I had made it and I had shrugged in response.

I finally flipped the paper over, only to see my destiny, written in black ink, scream up at me—seventy-two percent. "Wait, don't you need eighty percent to make it?" I wondered to myself. Then it had hit me—I had missed the cut-off by a mere eight percent.   I then made a vow to dance that much better so that the following year's tryouts would end differently…

Now, I found myself back in the same position as the year before. In keeping my vow, I had practiced non-stop ever since we had learned the dance. In an attempt to attain perfection, I had decided that for one week, Tapaires would come first before anything else, including my studies. I was determined to make the team at any cost.

When the day of reckoning arrived, nervous dancers once again surrounded me, stretching their anxious muscles in hopes of executing the highest kicks or hitting the lowest splits. We were briefed on the schedule and then given a sparkly sticker with a number on it. Then we all quietly filed out of the gym so the tryouts could commence. Sitting gingerly on the cold hallway floor, I stuck the sticker on my leo. Closing my eyes, I envisioned myself doing the dance perfectly endless times.

While waiting for my turn, I witnessed the same scenario repeatedly. Three people would go inside. Complete silence would dominate for two minutes and then the music would come on full-blast. Every time this happened, a few girls (myself included) would get up and dance just that one more time to get a feel for it. Then the girls would walk out the same way they walked in. They either came out incredibly pleased or so devastated that tears would quietly run down their faces…

Then, it was finally my turn. My two partners and I anxiously walked into the humid gym. There sat four Tapaire alumni, with looks of stone, prepared to decide our fates. The coach was also there, instructing us on what to do.

"Okay, jump-kick, jump-split," she instructed. We each took turns doing this move. Before going last, I took a deep breath and tried to relax. When the coach nodded at me, I did as we were taught—I put my arms out and made myself an inch taller. I prepped on the balls of my feet, and attempted the highest kick possible. Then I prepped again and forced my not-so-limber legs down into the splits. I wasn't all the way down. But nevertheless, I turned my head towards the judges and smiled—hoping that my charm would make up for my lack of flexibility.

After this nerve-racking task, the coach hit the play button on the stereo. In my beginning position, I struggled to remember the very first move. "Wait a minute…what is it?" I thought to myself. I had completely blanked!

But before I even had enough time to panic, the song, "Baby, I'm a Star," blared from the radio and my body automatically executed the right moves. I was so excited that energy seemed to just surge throughout my entire body. I felt indestructible. With a huge grin on my face, I danced just as I had earlier envisioned. I made no mistakes, did decent splits and kicks, and expressed so many facials that I thought I would run out of ones to do! After what seemed like only seconds later, I hit my last pose. A single drop of sweat ran slowly down my nose. I felt it linger along my face, but I never flinched. Confidently I walked out of that gym. All I could do now was sit and wait.

Finally, the last group was finished and the coach told us that the judges would be tabulating. Meanwhile, I sat with my friends and tried to act normal. Inside, however, I could feel the butterflies not only fluttering wildly in my stomach, but also flapping their wings so strongly that I actually felt nauseous.

The time arrived. Would my childhood dream come true? We walked together in the gym and I sat with two of my junior varsity teammates. Holding hands, we lowered our heads and waited for the verdict…

Finally the numbers of the lucky girls were rattled off. I did not register any of the numbers until I heard the coach say, "…One." I looked down at my sticker to ensure myself that the number one was written on it.

I had finally made the team! I was a Richfield Tapaire. My dream had become reality!

From there on I had three great years that I will never forget. Now that I am in college and the adventure has passed, I still think back to that fateful day and feel proud of what I had accomplished.

Brynn Erickson

International Cheer

Enthusiasm is life. ~Paul Scofield

We, the Linkoping Lightnings from Sweden, had earned a silver medal at last year's regionals. With the intention of defending our title from the year before, we gathered at six o'clock in the morning. Settling into the cars we began our trip to a town far away.

After a few hours, we arrived at the cottages we were to stay at in a small town whose name I had never heard before. After unpacking our things, we went to the competition hall.

We warmed up and went through the routine a couple times, twined tresses and put on our dresses. Then the competition began with the inauguration. They played "We Are The Champions". All around me there were cheerleaders. My only thought was, "This is life!"

The individual competition was first. One of our juniors, Soniya competed in this class. She was great! Fia and Mikaela competed next for us in the couple competition.

Then it was our time! We were competing in the Junior Cheer B class. We were the third out of five contestants to take the floor. We ran in and took our places on the mat. All the stunts and pyramids hit as they should. I was very happy! We kicked, yelled, jumped and run out.

The co-ed senior was the last class to compete. Our seniors competed and then the contest was done.

Each team picked one person to fetch the prize if selected. I was the lucky one. We waited for the distribution to start. I was on pins and needles, nervous to death.

At last the distribution started. They just announced the first, second and third place teams not the fourth or the fifth.

"Number 3..." they began to announce. I couldn't wait to hear the results. And when they didn't say our name, I thought that we had taken second.

"Number 2..." We weren't second either! We couldn't have been THAT bad! We didn't get any prize at all! I was very disappointed.

"Number 1..." Okay, who's the lucky one?

"The winner is Linkoping Lightnings!"

Hey wait a minute! That's us! Have we won?!

I screamed and yelled. I had the biggest smile on my face when I fetched the trophy and diploma. I was incredibly proud to be a member of the best junior team in the region!

Inga Ohman

A Dancer's Words of Wisdom

Ask yourself the secret of your success. Listen to your answer, and
practice it. ~**Richard Bach**

1. You must start at the bottom and work your way up.

2. Practice does not make you perfect. It just increases your chances of a wonderful performance.

3. Not all performances will go smoothly. You can always improve for the next one.

4. Always have something to improve on and work at. You will get better.

5. Smile—it will cover almost any mistake.

6. Take someone else's criticism toward another dancer into consideration. You might be able to improve as well.

7. Someone out there is always going to be better—you can't always be the best.

8. You might not always make the cut. Keep trying—your time will come.

9. If you love to perform, then perform. Don't let anyone tell you that you are not good enough.

10. If you want something bad enough, you will work for it.

11. Respect your fellow athletes. Most of them work just as hard as you do.

12. If you are on a team, act like it. Routines will not have the same feel if everyone acts like they're performing solos.

13. Gossip on a team hurts the whole team. Not just the person it's about.

14. You don't have to be best friends with everyone on the team. But get along with everyone; you will be spending a lot of time with them. It will bring the team down if there are arguments.

15. Problems need to be dealt with as they occur. Don't let them become distractions.

16. Your coach is there for a purpose. Listen, she knows what she is talking about.

17. You might get hurt one time or another; you will heal. Work harder to catch up.

18. Dreams are made to come true. Set a goal and reach for the stars!

Kristen E. Rasmussen

A Good Experience

The ultimate victory in competition is derived from the inner satisfaction of knowing that you have done your best and that you have gotten the most out of what you had to give. **~Howard Cosell**

Having won three first-place trophies at the Iowa State Drill Team Competitions, my co-director Marilyn and I reached the conclusion that we would really love to compete on the national level. After numerous fund-raisers and donations from our fans, we boarded a chartered bus and headed for Baltimore, Maryland and the NCA Danz Championship.

Marilyn and I had both said from the onset that we were going simply for the experience; we certainly did not expect to win. We would be gaining the adventure of competing at a higher level and of course, we would also be happy to see all the great sights of Washington D.C.

And sightsee we did! We stayed in a beautiful hotel in downtown Baltimore— merely walking distance from the harbor. We soaked up the sights like sponges. Just the pleasure we derived from that was enough to make the trip worth it!

The competition was held on Good Friday. When we arrived at the site, we were all slightly intimidated by the other teams, dressed in matching warm-ups, carrying garment bags and dragging racks of costumes. We had felt so proud just to have matching sweatshirts and newly purchased duffel bags proclaiming that yes, we were the Keokuk Iowa Little Feathers! Nevertheless, we weren't too intimidated to take on the escapade of competing and successfully performing in four categories—pom, dance, novelty, and prop.

After a lengthy and exciting competition, the award ceremony was to begin. Since we had been so busy getting dressed and getting on the floor at the correct time we really had no idea how the other teams had performed. Our parents seemed quite assured and impressed by our performances that they thought we would do well. However, we just looked at each other and convinced ourselves, that "yes, we just came for the experience."

As is our tradition, during the announcements of the place winners, we sit, holding each others's hands, with our heads bowed. We prayed while they announced the winners of the division that had gone before us. Then came Division III, our division…third place…not us. Well, maybe we placed second? Again not us. Marilyn and I let out huge sighs and let go of each other's hands.

"We're not going to win this thing," we said simultaneously.

"The Division II champions are…" said the announcer, "the Little Feathers from Keokuk, Iowa!"

Our whole group just erupted! We hugged, we laughed and we cried. We were going back to Keokuk with just a little more than the experience after all!

We were in such a frenzy that the announcer had to tell us to quiet down so that he could announce the Overall Winner from all three divisions. Oh what did we care? We had just won our division; the Overall Winner would be from one of those schools with the matching everything! We had won our division; who could possibly ask for more?

Amidst all the excitement, the announcer proceeded to call the place winners for the Overall category…third, second, and Overall Winner, or Grand Champion, or whatever they called it…Keokuk, Iowa! We were so busy savoring our division win that we almost missed it. We shared a moment of shocked silence as the idea of being chosen for this wondrous honor overwhelmed us. Marilyn and I were beyond thrilled. We were speechless. We were National Champions!!

Upon our return to the hotel, we promptly called our husbands back in Keokuk. When Marilyn's husband, who is incidentally the high school activity director at KHS, asked her how things went, Marilyn couldn't resist holding out on the suspense for just a little while longer. With tongue in cheek, she replied, "Not very well."

"Oh well," he said, "it was a good experience."

In answer to his response, she said, "Wes, we didn't JUST do very well; we did great; we won the darn thing!"

Of course he was as incredulous as my husband had been when I had called him. They knew all about the hard work that had gone into the trip and had in fact been right there along helping us.

When we arrived home to Keokuk, we were greeted by hundreds of well-wishers. On a fire truck, we rode down Main Street and on to the high school where the whole school and the city assembly awaited us.

I have to say that this was the most wondrous thing that I have ever been a part of. What a joy for Marilyn—having the chance to share such a blessed experience with her daughter, Nicky, captain of our dance team that year! Unfortunately, Marilyn died in August of 1993. I will miss her always and am thankful that we were able to share this magnificent event. Nicky, who is now a drill team director herself, and I still talk about that special time in our lives and yes, we are still a bit unbelieving.

The Little Feathers have won numerous state championships since that fateful day. These accomplishments, forever captured and recorded on banners, adorn the walls of the KHS fieldhouse right along side the one that will forever proclaim the Little Feathers as National Dance Champions 1988!

Fran Lukkarinen

One Last Time

"Remember tonight...for it is the beginning of always."

Friday night was the last time I had to do a lot of things. But as I cried, I realized that it symbolized a new beginning. For seven years I had cheered with the same group of guys and girls. Looking back, I remembered how we couldn't wait for our senior year, with the hopes that it would be our best year ever. Back then, we firmly believed that our boys, yes our boys, would be the football champions.

We had a special bond, we did, whether we realized it or not. Sure, there were those who just went through the motions and then there were those who gave it their all. Whatever group we belonged in, all our hearts were broken that night.

Secretly, yes, we all sighed, partly with relief, when it came to an end. But it was impossible to grip that after seven years, it was over. We cheerleaders were left only with the memories of the exciting games, the screaming fans, the competition, the mocking kids who mirrored our every move, and the pure adrenaline rush. These memories and our special friendships would surely last a lifetime.

As the lights flickered out in the stadium, we slowly walked off the field. In my heart, I knew that this was only a milestone and that I would soon go on to better. But for that moment, it was okay to cry.

Brooke Gruetzner

let's hear it for the boy!

The Squad Gods. They're big, they're strong -and they're cheerleaders."

Maine East High School, Coed Cheerleaders

The Male Cheerleader

"Any man can hold a girl's hand, but only the elite can hold her feet."

I am a cheerleader, no longer just a fan.

I am a cheerleader but also a man.

With a lot of practice and a little luck

Look at me now with a standing back tuck!

When I talk to the girls they say they would die

For the chance to stunt with just a few guys.

When stunting with my partner, it is me whom she trusts.

When she is falling, catch her I must.

I work very hard, practice night and day

No matter what the others call me, no matter what they say.

I am dedicated to cheerleading with everything I say and I do

As you and your sport, as dedicated as you.

When we talk to other athletes, all we want is respect--

Nothing more, nothing less, this is all that we request.

I am a cheerleader, boy do I make those girls fly!

And when they accidentally elbow me, I do not cry.

I have been punched, pushed and also shoved

When the stunts have fallen, this sport I still love.

I have been broken, have bled, and have even bruised

For the love of cheering; a love I won't lose.

I have found a sport from which I will never depart.

No matter what the gender, cheerleading comes from the heart.

Ross Kolodziej

I'll Be Back

A faithful friend is the medicine of life. ~Apocrypha

My first year on the squad, I worked diligently. With Nationals looming in our near future, I wanted to learn and master everything imaginable. One day at practice, with my peers' encouragement, I decided that it was about time that I knew how to execute a back tuck. Practicing on a large foam mat typically used by the high jumpers, I had no problem getting around. My teammates cheered me on and many offered their advice.

Well, it must have been one suggestion too many, because before I knew it, I found myself resting on the top half of the back of my neck. Apparently, having tried to incorporate all suggestions in one take, I jumped as high as ever but did not complete my rotation. For a brief instant, the fear I felt was overwhelmed by a numbness that encompassed my ears. But in spite of it, I got right back up, and continued practicing, writing off the terrific pain as whiplash. After another hour of practice with the usual bumps, kicks and falls common to a college co-ed squad, I went home to rest.

Aside from cheering at UTEP, I was also an Active Duty nurse for the Army. That very night I was scheduled to work a twelve-hour shift on the pediatric unit. Two and a half hours into my shift, my patients were all down for the night. Figuring it was as good a time as any, I decided to get something for the pain in my neck. I headed for the ER after assuring the other nurse on duty that I would be right back. Famous last words!

Once in the ER I did receive medication for my neck, but I was also persuaded to let them do an X-ray, "Just to be safe." The initial x-ray was marginally abnormal, so two more were taken. The second trip to X-ray revealed that I had pulled all the tendons from the top cervical spine and two from the second. I was immediately fitted for a collar and the orthopedic surgeon was called.

After a nice long chat with the ortho, my options were as follows: 1) do nothing, but if I sneezed or got hit in the head from behind, it would snap my spinal cord and I would die instantly, or 2) undergo surgery for a cervical fusion and screw fixation. Decisions, decisions. At 8:00 a.m. I went into surgery and was out by noon. So much for being right back!

I was released from the hospital at noon the following day…just in time for practice! My teammates' love and support confirmed what I had known all along--we were more than just a bunch of cheerleaders, we were a squad of friends.

Six weeks later I was freed from the neck brace. The doctors informed me that I could slowly get back into the swing of things, the rhythm of my normal routine.   For me, that entailed cheering. Despite several outside opinions, I felt that quitting at that point would only lead to many years of regret. Eight weeks after surgery I joined my team at the national competition and we finished sixth place.

Since my injury, I have heard of similar cases. However, none of the injured were fortunate enough to recover as quickly or as fully as I did. In retrospect, I feel I owe my recovery and my current outlook on life to the members of the UTEP Cheer Squad, my dearest friends. After that year, we went back to Nationals twice, finishing third both times.   Without a doubt the memories that we made together will be some of the greatest memories of my life. I thank God for them and for my life. I encourage others to share their lives and dreams together so that they may persevere and create lifetime memories.

Scott Poston

Pure Inspiration

"If it's in your heart, it shows in your spirit!"

I went to a football game at my school, with the sole intention of observing the cheerleaders to see if I wanted to try out. The cheer team consisted of a number of girls and a few boys. It must have been an "off" day for the squad—their spirit was at a low. Don't get me wrong, they definitely deserved respect for being out there on that cold night. It was pretty gloomy! They couldn't mask the fact that they weren't enjoying themselves. But who could blame them?

But as I continued to watch these girls and the boys cheer their football team on, one person especially caught my eye. This person was fantastic. Even though it was miserably cold, you would never have guessed it from how into cheering this person was. This cheerleader was totally getting into the routine, smiling his hardest and doing his best. While his teammates stiffly stood around, he put his all into each and every one of his moves. He was beyond cheerleading; he was pure inspiration.

People in the stands were talking about him and commenting on how weird he was. Still, that night, I never saw him without a smile on his face. To me, he was the true definition of a cheerleader. He gave it his all.

He is the inspiration and example I will follow when I try out for the squad. If he could cheer, shout and tumble, well then, hey, I should be so willing to cheer, shout and tumble with him! He definitely deserves all the respect and applause.

Ronda Slaughter

The Time of His Life

To succeed means that you may have to step out of line and march to the sound of your own drummer. ~Keith Degreen

Most people consider Drill/Dance an all-girl sport. That is until a guy, Bill Spata, tested the limits. With eight years of formal dance training in ballet, tap and jazz behind him, and no interest in playing either football or basketball, Bill concluded that on the drill team was where he wanted to be.

Everyone thought that his decision was a joke until one hundred girls and Bill showed up for the tryouts. Bill's friend Mike, a fellow dancer, had backed down the very last minute, leaving Bill to go it alone. And go it alone, he did!

First cuts…second cuts… and finally…the anticipated new team list was posted on the Athletic Director's door. School history was made that fateful eve when Bill's name appeared alongside twenty-three other female team members. Yes, the first male team member extraordinaire!

Controversy, doubt and even ridicule trailed Bill and his new position that first year. No one knew what to expect from the new male team member. One thing was for sure, Bill did not expect, nor did he receive any special treatment from coaches, captains or other team members.

Bill's captain and friend Beth was no stranger to Bill's dancing ability or potential. Bill and Beth had studied dance and competed together since they had both been eight years old. She knew that Bill expected self-perfection, knowing that he was to be the focal point amongst the sea of girls. With Bill's ideal in mind, Beth and the coaches would not settle for anything but excellence from him.

His dance skills and technique proved to be a real asset to the team. The girls tried harder to perfect their triple turns and their toe touches, just to keep up with him. Bill's unquestionable strength granted Beth and the rest of the team the opportunity to choreograph routines with partner work and lifts that had not been done before by other precision dance teams.

That first season, Bill gained the respect and recognition that he deserved. Undoubtedly, Bill had made an important breakthrough for the future of precision dance/drill teams. Stereotypes were broken. Devoted fans were made from previously dubious spectators. Numerous newspaper articles were written and two television specials were aired. Bill's team went on to win every state championship in every category that they entered. They received the highest scores in the State Championship's history.

To " The Time of My Life", from the movie "Dirty Dancing", Bill took the floor for the last time at the state competition. The team's Jazz/Dance routine took top honors and it was a befitting end to what had truly been the time of Bill's life.

Bill's drill team career ended with the state competition and the team banquet. His senior year was drawing to a close as well. His class honored him with the superlative "The Person who Did Most for his School" and crowned him as Senior Prom King. Because of his undying faith in himself and his team, Bill went from school joke to respected role model.

Following graduation, he was offered a scholarship from the nationally acclaimed River North Dance Co. in of Chicago. Dance team companies throughout the nation offered him jobs. Eagerly, Bill went to college in Arizona and toured each summer with Show Stoppers Drill Team Camps as an instructor.

Looking back at both his remarkable high school and college years, one could say that his self-confidence, his professional manner and his strong team presence were his claims to fame. He will always be remembered for opening the door for other male dancers and their aspirations to belong to dance/drill teams. To date, several Illinois dance teams have had male team members.

Whether you are male or female, however, the important thing that Bill gave to many, was the insight that no matter what sport you choose, you must realize your dream by seeing it; you must believe in your team and yourself by thinking it, and finally you must discipline yourself through hard work and team spirit to achieve it and you must never, ever give up!

Chris Spata

Never Give Up

"I don't play the field...I rule the sidelines!"

Looking at colleges, I initially considered some of the smaller ones in which I would be able to competitively play golf, basketball or baseball. I finally decided on one where I would be able to play basketball, but unfortunately it fell through. I then applied to Michigan State although I would most likely not make a team sport there. I got accepted and started in the fall of 1992.

During my first semester, I tremendously missed the team experience and the thrill of competition. At the end of that semester, I met a guy who was on the cheerleading team. After conversing with him, I was interested in getting involved. Hey—it was a team, and they competed...why not? He told me when and where the next tryouts were being held. He also advised me to work out and build muscle. Hmmm...

I had never done anything like it before. No gymnastics, no dance, and certainly no cheerleading. Although nervous, I decided to go for it. Tryouts were fun and I had a great time learning the stunts and the cheers. I made the first cut and felt that I had a good chance of actually making the team. However, during stunt practice three days before the final cuts, I tore my deltoid muscle while catching a flier falling from a stunt. I could barely move my arm and stunting was next to impossible. The trainers wrapped me up the best they could. Performing for final cuts was difficult and I lost a lot of points. My number would not appear on the team list.

During the rest of the year, I worked out in preparation for the following year's tryout. I was determined to make it. When they rolled around I was confident that this was my chance. First cuts went smoothly, and I again found myself moving on to the final round.

Looking around the room, I was sure that there was a spot for me on the team. But as luck would have it, the difficult practices took a toll on my body. This time I pulled tendons in my wrist. Again, I was taped to keep it from moving. Stunting felt as if I had knives stuck in my wrist. I still hoped for the best—maybe the coach would see how well I was doing despite my injury and still put me on the team. But no, my number was missing from the list once again.

I had all but given up. I had convinced myself that another tryout would not only be embarrassing, but also a waste of time. When tryouts rolled around again, I handed out many excuses to those who asked me if I was up for the challenge. But wouldn't you know it, the first day of tryouts I found myself pulling out my good old workout clothes and heading to the gym.

There were no expectations this time; I had already experienced failure and disappointment two times too many. I approached tryouts in an entire new way. I looked as it as a way to enjoy myself rather than a self-measure of success. That way, I still worked hard but this time, without the pressure. I reminded myself that through Christ I could do all things.

The practices seemed to fly by. Like the previous two times, I made first cut. Even though I was excited to move onto the next round, I had to get over one more hurdle—injuries, or in this case, the lack of them!

The night of final cuts finally arrived and there were no injuries or excuses to be found! I gave myself a minute of reprieve before the finals began and prayed that "God's will be done and allow me to have fun. He will surely get the credit for even giving me the strength to just be a part of such a wonderful thing." A calming feeling came over me and the final round went smoothly...

The next morning I made the walk I had made before. This time, as I walked up the stairs to the postings, I asked, "God, give me wisdom, and the ability to deal with whatever the results are, in a Christian way." Gazing at the list, I found my number. After three trying years, I had finally made the cheerleading team.

I was a part of the Michigan State Cheer Team for three years. My second year we took fourteenth at Nationals. Since my college cheer career, I have coached and performed with a U.S. team in Brazil. I have choreographed high school competition routines and have even trained others who are hoping to make their college cheer teams.

In the world of cheer, it can be a hard row to hoe for a man. But believing in yourself and having faith makes anything possible. NEVER GIVE UP!

Tyson Ferguson

Homecoming

Adversity teaches a man about himself. ~Alonzo Mourning

I remember it like it was yesterday...I was so excited over the cheerleading tryouts. Who would make it? Who would represent the school?

Finally, the day of cheerleading tryouts arrived, and yes, I made it! I was so excited, but my father, on the other hand, saw things differently. He wasn't the only one. From a small Texan town, people did not understand why I would want to be on the team. They couldn't comprehend the fact that yes, males could be cheerleaders....

On the very day our uniforms were to be issued, my father said, "NO." No, to me being a cheerleader. I was devastated. Looking back, I know he was just trying to keep me from having to endure the snide remarks, and the associated "gay" stigma of a male cheerleader.

Good intentions or not, his decision made that year the hardest one of my life. I sat at every cheer-rally that fall and imagined myself cheering. Actually, that wasn't even the hardest part...telling people that I could not cheer because my dad said so was. Sometimes I think he was embarrassed, or ashamed.

Yet, I persisted. I talked to my dad just about every day about the situation, and I explained to him that being a cheerleader was not just a female role. Finally, three days before the eighth grade tryout he said, "Fine, do it. But if you get hurt, well..."

I was so excited. I remember the tryout, all of those people...well, I did make it, and let me tell you, it was the best feeling....

The following fall, however, I finally understood what my dad had been talking about...

All the snide remarks and the nicknames—'Tinker Bell', or my favorite- 'F-A-G'. It seemed to get worse as the season went on. Yet, my teammates, who to this very day are still good friends of mine, never let me give up. They would tell their football-playing boyfriends that they needed "to get in touch with themselves", or that they were just jealous!

My freshman year, I tried out for the high school squad. Oh my, you will never know how scared I was... all of those high school football players! What would they say?

What would they think? Regardless, I told myself to suck it up, stick it out, and to just do it!

As expected, it was very difficult and the remarks were harsh and painful, but I convinced myself to get over it. Cheerleading was a major part of my high school education. I went on and made Junior Varsity and then Varsity. I was even fortunate enough to be named an 'All American Cheerleader.'

After graduating from high school, schools came a-calling…I went on and cheered for two Division I schools and one Division II School--all on cheerleading scholarships!

Today, I am a teacher, back in my hometown. Yes in my hometown, and yes, you better believe it-- "I am the Cheerleading Coach." Yes, there are still people who question what I do, but my girls are so great, they just keep plugging along.

I never gave up, and I always told myself that there was nothing in this world that I could not have or obtain. For certain, the harsh words and the disappointment may be plentiful, but all who have spirited souls can do it. Granted, my father never saw me cheer, even when I was in college, but I know he is very proud to say that I am the Hometown Cheerleading Coach...

David Tamez

making it big

When you reach for the sky, you land amongst the stars."

Photo courtesy of David Silverman/New England Patriots

As Good As It Gets!

***There was simply from this quite early age the awareness that the only thing I wanted was to dance.** ~Rudolf Nureyev*

When I was nine, I watched them cheer--
Those older girls of ten.
I couldn't wait until next year
So I could join right in.

I made the team & made dear friends
I thought we were *so cool...*
There was no sadness to see it end...
I headed for high school.

Four years brought both pride and tears
Hard work - Defeat – Success.
And at the end of senior year
I looked toward the best.

Memphis State was 'Number One'
The year I joined the team.
I loved the coach - I loved the crowd
And now - I'd lived my Dream.

And still ... I dreamed of dancing pro
An avid Raider Fan.
I traveled back to Oakland
Feeling fit and feeling tan.

Tryouts were the toughest yet-
500 women strong.

A grueling two weeks later
They took **me** along!

To be a part of this great team
To dance before this crowd
To hear the Raider Anthem
I'd never felt so proud.

Awards are part of any team
And in my second year
<u>My</u> name was called when they announced
'Raiderette - Of the Year'.

Looking back on all I've done
I've had but one regret
And that's the need to enjoy--
<u>THIS</u> IS AS GOOD AS IT GETS...

BE SATISFIED WHEREVER YOU ARE!!

Julie L. Grogan

Chubby Girl with Pink Glasses

The most distinguishing feature of winners is their intensity of purpose.
~Alymer Letternman

I'm writing this story for all the little girls who think they are unpopular, unattractive, or "nerdy". It's for the girls who are teased by others, overlooked by boys, and pessimistic about their goals and dreams because of how they perceive themselves. I can relate to these girls because I used to be one of them.

In grade school I epitomized the typecast nerd. I had tightly permed hair that couldn't help but lay lopsided on my head. I wore pink glasses. I was so overweight, I had to wear the "pretty plus" elastic jeans. I always found myself wishing to be the most beautiful and popular girl in my class. But what I wished for most of all was to be a cheerleader.

At every hometown parade, I sat front row and center on the curb, just to catch a glimpse of the pompon girls bouncing by. I attended the high school cheerleading clinics with great excitement. I often found myself performing in front of my mirror, pretending I was the head cheerleader at a basketball game. Thoughts of being a cheerleader occupied my life, but I had already given up hope. I did not look like a cheerleader.

In both the 7th and 8th grades I unsuccessfully auditioned for the team. Of course I went home both times and cried my eyes out. In high school, however something great happened... I grew taller, my tight hair loosened, and I stopped wearing those darn pink glasses! With renewed hope and a new sense of self-esteem, I tried out for the pompon squad my sophomore year. Even though I tripped constantly all over my own feet and was always a count behind everyone, someone must have seen potential in me because I made it!

For the next two years, I spent countless nights in my driveway practicing routines. By my senior year, I was the captain. Yes, the once chubby girl with pink glasses had become the captain!!

But what lay ahead of me proved to be a greater challenge....

The Los Angeles Rams Football organization had just moved to St. Louis, and like the long-gone little girl with the pink glasses, I watched their glamorous cheerleaders from the sidelines. With great fear and excitement, I realized what my next goal was to be...

The next year, I went to the Rams' cheerleader tryouts and discovered that I just wasn't quite ready for the challenge. The other girls had the right make-up and coiffed hair, danced with perfection, and knew what to say and how to act. I felt myself reverting back to that awkward and overlooked little girl. I wanted to crawl right into a hole! All I could do was put on a smile and do the best I could. I didn't make it, but I was definitely not going to give up.

Over the course of the next year, I did everything I could to become that "complete package." I learned how to present myself, to put on makeup, and to do my hair. I learned to be proud of myself and to show my pride in the way that I walked.

The next year, I again went to the tryouts and, yes, I made it! Yes, that once chubby girl with pink glasses had become a St. Louis Rams Cheerleader. So...to all those little girls who think their looks hold them back from reaching their dreams, I'm your proof that dreams can indeed come true.

Amy Reiter

Break A Leg!

"Hi! My name is Linda Smith, and I'm #30..."

Sound familiar? Anyone who has experienced the audition process can relate to the excitement, adrenaline, and yes, the inevitable anxiety that courses throughout your entire body as you are about to step onto the audition stage!

The number 30 has special meaning for me. It was the number I had carefully pinned to my audition outfit the year I was finally selected to the New England Patriots Cheerleading Squad! Like many years prior, I had spent the year perfecting everything in preparation for auditions. I had taken classes to gain experience in quickly committing dance combinations to memory. Again, I had diligently practiced kicks, splits, and had gone through the ritual of selecting "the perfect" audition outfit. This, however, was the year that my perseverance would pay off!

Auditioning for the New England Patriots Cheerleading Squad had become somewhat of an annual event for me. Each year I would anxiously await the arrival of the audition packet in the mail. Although I had auditioned for the team on previous occasions and had been overlooked, I was always hopeful that the current year would be "the year!" I began to view auditions as such that, regardless of the outcome, it would leave me with greater wisdom and valuable experiences. I always came away with wonderful new friends, exciting dance combinations, effective workouts, and of course, invaluable practice for the following year's audition.

The belief that we are responsible for our life choices was deeply instilled in me by my family. In this case I realized that I had two choices - to give up (in which case I would never achieve my goal), or to maintain a positive attitude and to keep trying! Had I not chosen the second choice, I would never have had the treasured memory of the day I was selected and welcomed to The New England Patriots Cheerleading Squad!

The happiness of seeing other individuals selected to the team, after faithfully returning year after year to audition, is one of the greatest rewards that I have experienced as a veteran NFL Cheerleader. Understandably, I share a special connection with those with such perseverance!

This past year, a particular Rookie on the team approached me and wholeheartedly thanked me for my constant encouragement. The year before she had made the team, I had shared many of my audition experiences with her, with hopes that it would give her the courage to persevere. The following year she did return, and made the team! What a wonderful feeling—for both her and me!

A world of opportunities awaits you! Select those of interest and commit yourself to attaining your goals by practicing perseverance and maintaining a positive attitude. As we dancers say…break a leg!

Linda Michelle Smith

Here Lady

No matter what age you are, or what your circumstances might be, you are special, and you still have something unique to offer. ~Barbara De Angelis

As cheerleaders for the New England Patriots, we make many appearances at local charities, events, and clubs. After leaving a Monday night football event, I had a spot of car trouble. I found a nearby pay phone along the side of the busy Boston street.

I stood at this pay phone searching for change. While seeking out coins, I spied a homeless person across the street. He stood there, speaking to himself, while banging a plastic bottle on his head. Still scrambling for change, I noticed he was slowly walking over to me.

I was so scared. With a dirty face and shabby clothes just hanging off of him, he continued to approach me.

I repeat, I was so scared.

Upon reaching me, he held out a shaking hand, clad in a ripped glove. In it he held one dime and one penny.

"Here lady," he said.

April Fitch

I Can Do This!

They can because they think they can. ~Virgil

June 1984. An ad placed in the Star Tribune called for women interested in trying out for the first-ever professional Minnesota Vikings Cheerleading Team.

"I can do this!" I thought to myself. So I quickly typed up my resume, attached my photo and sent it to the Vikings office. A few weeks later I received an invitation to try out for the team.

Driving down to the Metrodome I anticipated a crowd of 100 women or so vying for 36 positions. Did I have a shot? Maybe. Would it be fun? Definitely!

I pulled into the parking lot and sat in my car for nearly thirty minutes, watching all the beautiful women enter the dome. There had to be over 300 people walking in! On first impression alone, I had already selected 'the team'. Did I still think I had a shot? No. Was I scared to death? Yes!

"But hey, I'm here," I said to myself. "I got invited. So I'm going to go in with the attitude that this will be fun. I probably won't make it but hey ... at least I can say that I was there!"

Well, to my surprise, there were over 600 candidates. Talk about having a rock in your gut! I almost turned right around and walked out the door. But I didn't. I walked up, got my number (#262), and proceeded to enter the dome.

Susan Anderson, the coach of the new squad, a well-known studio owner and exceptional dancer, quickly taught us our tryout routine. I had a hard time getting it down but I still gave it my best shot. I thought since my last name began with a 'K' that I'd have plenty of time to practice while the others began the tryout procedure.

That is, until they announced over the loud speaker, "We are going to begin with the K's." My heart sank. I remained on the field while they went through groups of ten. Too soon for my liking, my group was announced.

I didn't know the routine well enough. I thought about walking away right then and there. Until one of the Viking staff members said, "You can do it. Give it a shot."

With God watching over me, I slowly walked forward with my group and performed the routine. I can honestly say I don't remember the performance at all! It was one big blur. We began. We finished. We walked off the field. That was it.

~   ~   ~

The Vikings Staff gave us a phone number to call to see if we had made the first cut. A voice announced the numbers of the top 100 candidates who would advance into the semi-final round. Outside my home, high on a hill, I sat with my portable phone. Repeatedly dialing the number over and over, I found it constantly busy (of course). I finally made it through!

"... 254, 258, 262..."

262! They said my number! Wow! I did it! I started to jump up and down and scream. My sister came running and asked, "Are you okay? What's wrong?"

I screamed, "I made it to the semi-final round! I did it! I did it!" Now I really wanted it bad. I was determined to make the team.

~   ~   ~

The last cut took place a week later. Each candidate auditioned individually on the huge field. One by one, we anxiously performed the routine Sue Anderson had just taught us only moments earlier. One by one, the judging panel evaluated our performance. We were then interviewed on the spot.

The final decision was made. Who would make the team?

~   ~   ~

A week or so later I received a letter in the mail. I clearly remember the envelope. "Minnesota Vikings" marked the upper left-hand corner. This was *the* 'sorry to inform you' or 'congratulations' letter. Which would it be?

"Congratulations. We are happy to inform you that you have been chosen as one of the first-ever professional cheerleaders for the Minnesota Vikings."

I *can* do this!

Lisa Kubinski Saline

Ups and Downs

The first task of a leader is to keep hope ali

KC Rangerette Captain Overcomes Defeat

Shannon Harty has looked defeat square in the face and

As the 1999-2000 captain of the Kilgore College Rangerettes from Kilgore,

original and still most prestigious dance/drill team in the world, she held a leadership

position envied by many a young lady who aspires to be a Rangerette.

But it wasn't an easy road for Ms. Harty. It was more than just a little bit bumpy, too. Just two years earlier, she found herself confronting doubts that she would ever fulfill her dream of even being a Rangerette.

It was first in the summer of 1997 that she tried out for the team. Fresh out of Allen High School in Allen, Texas, where she was an officer of the Tallonettes her junior year and captain her senior year, she attended the Rangerette's summer camp and the grueling process leading up to tryouts. Like the other hopefuls, she sat on the stage of Dodson Auditorium anxiously waiting for the traditional announcement of the new squad members--the lowering of the sign with the tryout numbers printed of those who made the squad.

As the sign was lowered, she searched frantically for her number. It wasn't there. She hadn't made it. She was not a Rangerette.

"It was a shock," she now recalls vividly. "It was the first thing that I had ever tried out for that I really wanted, and I didn't make it. I had been pretty lucky up to that point."

Returning home to Allen without the red, white and blue uniform was difficult, she admits. "I was a little embarrassed," she said. "Everybody at home knew that I was trying out (for Rangerettes). It just sort of snowballed."

In addition to having to deal with the disappointment of not making the Rangerettes, she also had to decide what she was now going to do. "I had three days to figure out where to go to college. I had no idea what I was going to do with my life. I

...me and talked to my parents, and then decided to go to Richland College, where ...ance teacher was, and to take classes there."

Three days after not making the Rangerettes, on a date she still remembers, Ms. Harty decided she was going to try out for Rangerettes yet again. "I remember, it was Aug. 23, and I told my parents that I was going to try out again. I knew that it was what I was supposed to do. I wasn't going to be happy doing anything else."

So all through the fall of 1997 and spring of 1998, Ms. Harty took classes at Richland College and practiced with her dance instructor. When the summer of 1998 arrived, she again attended Rangerette Camp and pre-training. Once again she found herself sitting on the stage of Dodson Auditorium, anxiously waiting for the sign to be lowered and knowing all too well the feelings she would have if her number (# 51) wasn't on the sign. She recalled the feelings she had had at the same time the year before.

And she remembered how it felt to sit in the stands at the football stadium that previous fall and watch the Rangerettes perform, knowing that it was the one performing group she had dreamed so long to be a member of. And she remembered how long the past year had felt as she waited for tryouts to come around again.

Finally, the sign was lowered and number 51 was on it. She had made it. She was a Rangerette. Her dream had come true.

Ms. Harty embraced her role as a Rangerette, even though her freshman year was filled with many ups and downs. She was selected as freshman class sergeant, the top freshman leadership position selected by the other freshman Rangerettes. That was definitely an up.

But she got to perform in only one game her freshman year, and that was as a last-minute substitute. That was a down.

In January of her freshman year, she auditioned for the Swingsters, a division of Rangerettes that dances at events and functions where a smaller group is more appropriate. She did not make it.

"There were a couple of days afterward where I threw a pity party," she said of the disappointment. "I finally asked myself, 'Did you try out for Rangerettes to be a Swingster, or did you try out to be a Rangerette?' I had to quit feeling sorry for myself. It was hard, though."

Then, at the beginning of her sophomore year, she tried out for Officer.

"The dancing and the kicking have always been challenges for me," she said. "But leadership skills always come easy for me. I told myself when I made Rangerettes that I would become involved as much as I could, so I did."

Ironically, Ms. Harty's first time to ever perform the Rangerettes' trademark high kick routine at their home stadium, the R.E. St. John Stadium, was that fall. And she performed it as captain of the group.

"There seemed to be a plan for me that some things didn't happen the way I wanted them to, but it all worked out," she said.

It worked out again on August 20 when she tried out for one of five officers, and not only made Officer, but made Captain.

According to Dana Blair, director of the Rangerettes, Ms. Harty served the role of Rangerette captain very well. "She was extremely mature, beyond words," said Ms. Blair. "She was very efficient and I trusted her completely. She could really run the team and I knew she could handle any situation. I would take a million more just like her."

With the Rangerettes celebrating their 60th anniversary the year Ms. Harty became captain, the role of the leadership position became more important, according to Ms. Blair. "There was a lot more publicity related to the anniversary, and when that came along we steered the media towards her when they wanted to talk to a Rangerette. She was a great captain."

But while the limelight shone on her and the Rangerettes that year, Ms. Harty never forgot what she went through to get there. In retrospect, she feels that her "failures" were valuable learning opportunities.

"I was not ready to be a Rangerette the first time around, at all. I'm glad they didn't pick me the first time. I'd have missed out on so much, and wouldn't have had such great friends like I now have."

She admits that having to try harder to become a Rangerette gave her a better appreciation for being one. " I know what it's like to sit at home, and to watch performances from the stands. I hope I appreciated (being a Rangerette) a lot more. I tried to."

After becoming captain, Ms. Harty again had an 'up' cycle. Not only did the group celebrate their 60th anniversary, but they also traveled to Ireland where they participated in St. Patrick's Day celebrations.

Ms. Harty said one of her goals in life is to make use of the knowledge she acquired over the past two years to help others. "I want to be a drill team director while I'm young and coming out of the experiences I have had. I have so much to offer. I have a good base. I hope I never forget what it is like not to make something. I've gotten to see both sides.

"I think I'm really lucky. Before I was 21 I had more great experiences than some people have in an entire lifetime. If things continue like this, I'm sure I'm in for some more excitement!"

Doug Wintermute

Note: Shannon Harty is scheduled to graduate from Sam Houston University in Huntsville, Texas with a Bachelor of Arts degree in dance. After graduation, she will move to Austin, Texas where she will become the assistant director and choreographer to the Hyline Dance Team at Westlake High School. She will also teach dance classes.

Lucky Seven

If at first you don't succeed, try, try, try again. ~W. E Hickson

1991.   On my way to work one day, I heard a radio advertisement announcing the auditions for the New England Patriots Cheerleaders. The Patriots had not had a cheerleading team for several years, so I thought... WOW, wouldn't that be a neat thing to do?! Living in the area and being an avid football fan, I adored the Patriots as my #1 team. To cheer for them, boy, now that would be living the ultimate dream!

So I went to the audition and didn't make it past the first cut.   I had never auditioned for anything like this before, so I was far from discouraged. It had been fun to just try out for the team! I was inspired... next year would be different... that would be the year I'd make it.

1992.   Adorned in a better outfit (red/white/blue, of course!) and a little experience under my belt, I made it past the first cut, but... not past the second. Yes, I was a little disappointed. I thought it would be an easy process, but when you have 300 other talented women trying out, it turned out to be not so easy. I just reminded myself that I had done better than I had the previous year.

As my quest for success continued, I asked myself what I could possibly do different, what could I do better? Better look? Better hairstyle? BETTER DANCING!! That was the ticket-- I'd take dance classes! Unlike many of the other dancers, I did not have a formal dance training background. So I took a Modern Jazz class. It was fun; it was for a purpose! I was determined to do better at the next audition. Dancing all year long would help me for that one day when I needed it the most.

1993. I made it to the Final Auditions!! I had a personal interview with the coach and everything. I was so excited. And quickly disappointed as well-- I didn't make the first cut at Finals... didn't make it to that final round where you are no longer a number, but a member of the team. Oh, I longed to hear my name called! At that moment, I said to myself, "Don't they know how good I would be if they would just put me on the team?" So, I figured three times in a row – it's just not meant to be. I'll stop auditioning.

Then 1994 came, and I just didn't have it in me to really stop trying. I thought, "What if this is my year, if I don't try, I'll never know… and I've got nothing to lose". So I tried, and again, I made it to Finals but not past that first cut.

Understandably, many people were surprised when I tried out 4 times and didn't make it, 5 times and didn't make it, 6 times (in a row I might add) and didn't make it. Was I crazy? Maybe, but, I believed I could do it! It was tough because every time I walked through those doors I would always wonder if people thought I was weird for coming back again… "Oh, there she is, <u>again</u>", I imagined everyone saying. On the other hand, I always felt I had more to offer and that I could be better onstage than I had the year before.

Friends and family always stood behind me – so excited for me to try – and then disappointed with me when I didn't make it. They were my biggest fans! The Patriots Cheerleaders I met were always so supportive and friendly whenever they saw me… who wouldn't want to be on a team like that? Then, one day I happened to bump into one of the cheerleaders at a local restaurant. She remembered who I was and approached me! Hearing that I was not going to audition for a 7th time, she was surprised and encouraged me to try, at least one more time. There was going to be many spots open for the new season. Then it started… my wheels started to turn again… just when I thought I was done putting myself through this grind!

1997. I showed up ready to go, and was once more astonished that people didn't find me crazy for trying <u>again</u>! I made it to the Finals (my 4th time there) and with my whole family watching, I actually heard my number called to proceed to the next and final round! If nothing else, I was psyched to make it to that round.

As we learned that final dance routine, I felt so confident about every move I made, I had so much fun… a feeling I hadn't experienced at such a level. Then, when the judges reappeared after what seemed like forever, the coach of the Patriots Cheerleaders began calling the names.

Then I heard it, "and next, Catherine Frechette!"

I stood up, in shock, had she just called my name? Me? I quickly ran up on stage and proceeded to give 'My Coach' a big hug. She said to me, "Seven times, huh?"

And I replied… "Seven is my lucky number!"

I finally did it. I had made it. I was part of the NFL; I was a Patriots Cheerleader! It was the greatest moment; my whole family was there to share in the joy and excitement! What a great gift to give them! I knew I was part of something special when the son of the New England Patriots' owner approached me. He shook my hand, welcomed me to the team, and congratulated me on my persistence! Wow!

Now, in my third year with the Patriots Cheerleaders, I look back on every minute. I cherish every moment. I never imagined that being a part of this team would be so rewarding. Every Game Day I get to share my excitement for the Patriots with 60,000 other fans... at appearances I can put a smile on someone else's face or add a little sparkle to their day!

Our whole team is a big family. We enjoy being together and miss each other when we're apart. We continually strive to be the best team that we can be. Being a veteran, you must audition every year at Finals to earn your position back. The hard work never ends! I strive to be my best everyday and I never take anything for granted.

I believed in myself, and I didn't give up. To all those out there with a dream... you must <u>trust</u> in yourself that you CAN do it, and you must <u>believe</u> in yourself that you WILL do it... with that and a little luck, your dreams can come true! No matter what happens, you can walk away knowing you did your best!

Cheers!

Catherine Frechette Healey

Dedication to a Dream

Excellence is the gradual result of always striving to do better.
~Pat Riley

One of my jobs as an NFL Cheerleader Director is to organize and prepare for the auditions. My first year as the director for the San Francisco 49ers Cheerleaders I held a workshop prior to the auditions, designed to help women attain their dreams of becoming part of our team. Hundreds of women attended this class. Each one wanted to master every aspect of how to be successful in their dancing endeavors.

At the actual audition that year, there were many hopefuls: women who attended the workshop, women who didn't, and veterans from the previous year. As the tryout process continued, I naturally observed many hopefuls get eliminated. I also noticed that the women who had attended the workshop were better than the others that hadn't. At that point I made a mental note to spend more time, in future years, on the workshop and with the women that attended.

The advent of the next season came very quickly and I held true to my promise. Now however, there were six workshops, and each was booked. As I signed in the attendees for a particular workshop, I detected a familiar face. The face belonged to a woman who had attended the workshop the previous year. Her name was Janice. I remembered her because she had an extremely beautiful smile and was very eager to learn.

At auditions, the room filled with hundreds of women. In groups of three, they learned and performed difficult combinations in front of the judges. I, of course, promptly spotted Janice. The difficult dance number was really pushing her to her limit. However, she stayed with the group and made it through the routine--smile and all. After the hundreds had been judged, I read off the numbers of those dancers who were to stay for the next round. I didn't realize until much later that Janice's number had not been called.

Year Three rolled around and once again, it was time for the workshops. During sign-in, I looked up from my list to see Janice. She said, " Hi, do you remember me?" Of course I did.

"I have been taking dance classes all year to prepare for the audition," she remarked. Sure enough, her hard work had paid off. Undoubtedly, she stood out amongst the other women in the class. I was deeply impressed by her perseverance.

The usual intimidating scene played itself out at auditions. Hundreds of women, dressed to kill in their rhinestone-studded outfits, leaped and turned across the floor. All were ready to compete for a spot on our famous team. Janice looked beautiful in her sparkly outfit (She had really been taking notes!).

With the others, Janice learned the first combination and performed it well--well enough to make the first cut! The second dance combination was then taught to the group. The judges couldn't help but to love her and she made it to Finals. But the final audition came and went and Janice still hadn't made the team.

Year Four. There I was, back at the workshop, signing people in. As in previous years, there was Janice, ready to learn, practice and prepare. Once again she told me she had taken dance classes all year, had been working out at a gym, and had attended games just to watch the cheerleaders. Her unrelenting desire and efforts to achieve what was very important to her amazed me.

Entering the auditions that year must have been hard for Janice. She had learned and prepared for three years, but was it ever going to be enough? Once again hundreds of 49er Cheerleader hopefuls, decked out in coiffed hair and stage makeup, showed up to compete for the few cherished spots. Walking into that room would be intimidating enough for someone who had been on the team for five years, let alone someone who had been disappointed year after year!

Through it all though, Janice kept her chin up and a smile on her face. Some of the team's veterans had gotten to know Janice and were duly impressed by her determination. They even cheered for her as she performed the tough dance routine in front of the judges. Unsurprisingly, she made it through all the preliminary cuts and once again made it to Finals. During Finals, she was nothing short of amazing. She sparkled like I had never seen her sparkle before--there was no doubt in anyone's mind - Janice was going to be a 49ers Cheerleader! And indeed, that year she had finally made the team.

I was so touched by Janice's story that I shared it with the new team at our Mini-Camp. As I was telling the tale, I purposely omitted her name. She didn't even realize that I was talking about her until I said, "...and that courageous person is sitting with us here in this room."

Just as I said those words she quietly brought her hand to her chest and whispered, with tears in her eyes, "Me?"

I nodded and said, "'Yes, Janice it's you."

As I glanced around the room I noticed there wasn't a dry eye. The rest of the team was just as touched by her dedication and hard work as I had been. That very moment I realized that if you don't know what your goals are, then you will never know if and when you can truly achieve them. With hard work and dedication, though, you can, and will.

Angela King-Twitero

Making It Big

"Sacrifice is giving up something good for something better."

From the very first moment my chubby little foot stepped onto the floor of a dance studio, I knew that I was meant to be there. Dancing is my passion and since the age of three, I have always known that I was meant to express myself through it. During the rough spots in my life, when I would question my sanity, dancing has constantly given me the power to put things back into perspective.

Becoming pregnant at the age of eighteen, right out of high school, has definitely been the roughest spot yet. My dreams of dancing professionally crumbled before my eyes and I was devastated. I thought that I had ruined my life. My parents, though disappointed in me, were nothing but supportive. They made it perfectly clear that "family sticks together".

Four months into my pregnancy, I was obligated to dance and give away a title that I had won the previous year. Determined, I did dance at that competition and did give away my title but much to my dismay, did not perform well. The defining and lowest point in my life soon followed. After the performance, reality hit. My life as I had known it was over. I found a quiet corner and sobbed.

I continued to dance recreationally throughout my pregnancy but dancing was bittersweet. It represented everything that I would never be. I went through a period of postpartum depression but my family helped me to pull through. They picked up the pieces that I let fall and they gave me the strength and courage to begin auditioning again.

I didn't waste time with the 'small stuff.' I went directly to the Orlando Magic Dancers Audition three and a half months after I had given birth to my son. I made it to the final cut and the interview process, only to be let go.

I was disappointed but exhilarated at the same time. I had tapped into new energy! My family continued to help me build up my confidence. By the following year, I was more than ready to go. So ready in fact, that I made it!

When I called from the auditorium to inform my family, my dad started to cry. I got a hold of my mother at her family's house and she was so overjoyed that she also started to cry! Later that day, my sister confided that my father had visited all our neighbors, knocking on their doors to inform them that his daughter was an Orlando Magic Dancer! At that moment, he was more proud of me than he was embarrassed by his own wild antics!

I'm into my third season with the Magic. Next semester I will graduate with my Bachelor's Degree. I teach dance classes in the evenings and also dance with a number of production companies around Florida.

My son is a happy, well-adjusted three-year old. He is the light of my life and I wouldn't go back and change anything. I owe so much to my proud and loving family. To this day, my family comes to every Orlando Magic game that they possibly can (sometimes, Dad will buy tickets off of someone on the street just to be there).

Little did I know on that day when I was sobbing in that solitaire corner, that my life was just beginning and that yes, life as I knew it then ***was indeed*** over. Life, however, as I know it now is far greater than I ever could have imagined.

I cannot even begin to take credit for everything I have accomplished because, as my parents said on that fateful day four years ago, "Family sticks together." We are reaping the rewards that come only from a loving and supportive family that builds each other up and inspires one another to reach for the stars and follow dreams wherever they may lead!

I now have a different perspective on 'making it big'. I realize that when someone fulfills a dream, they rarely, if ever, do it on her own. There is most always a support system behind them rooting for them, especially during the tough times. 'Making it big' isn't about being a 'star', it is about humility and realizing how you got there and, most of all, appreciating the people who let you shine.

Brandy Daimwood

Auditions

"A winning smile makes winners of us all."

Walk in the door

What do I see?

Hundreds of eyes

Staring right at me.

Some hold confidence,

Others look scared.

At least there are a few here

With the feelings I share.

I scan the room

For a familiar face—

A warm smile, a friend,

But there's not a trace.

My heart starts to beat faster;

My palms begin to sweat

And I haven't even

Signed in at the welcome table yet!

Approaching the table

I'm greeted with a smile.

A veteran cheerleader

Finds my file.

She makes me feel welcome,

Introduces herself with a grin.

It's amazing how a smile

Makes you feel you fit in.

She gives me a number

And hands me some sheets.

"Sign here and here," she points,

"Be sure that it's neat.

Then head to that man

For a Polaroid shot.

It'll be your first impression;

So give it all

That you've got.

Now don't be nervous,

Have confidence and…

Believe in yourself—

You need to know that you can.

Each woman that's here

Has as good a chance as any.

So don't hold yourself back

And you'll stand out

Amongst the many."

So I heeded her directions

Headed straight for the man

Who took my photo

And placed it in my hand.

Onto the next station

I walk and think on the way—

Keep confident, smile

And I'll go home a cheerleader today.

The music begins

The routine looks tough

Will giving it all that I've got

Be enough?

Stay focused, concentrate,

Make it look easy—

Be energetic, exciting,

But avoid looking cheesy.

First cuts were called

One by one the girls dropped.

Who would have guessed she'd call my name

Before she had stopped?

My muscles are tired;

My body feels sore.

Another routine starts

Out on the floor.

I thought the last one was tough

But this one is worse—

With a funky combination

Done forward and then in reverse.

Please don't let my feet

Get ahead of my mind!

We're judged on the steps

And I must keep in time.

Sixteen high kicks,

A split and more smiles.

I'm done with Round Two

And I finish with style.

Final cuts are announced.

Oh my goodness, could it be?

That's my name she just called.

I raise my hand—"That's me!!"

I knew I could do it

In my heart all along.

But sometimes my mind

Just gets it all wrong.

Now next year at auditions,

I'll know what to do—

Be the smile at the table

And help another hopeful through.

For it was that veteran at the table
Who did it for me—
Reminded me to believe in myself
And become what I wanted to be.

Tracie J. Guenette

Last Dance

"And what do you think is your ultimate goal? I should think a nice little dance in heaven."

Becoming a member of the Orlando Miracle M-Squad for its inaugural season was the most powerful experience of my life.   Forever changing my being, it gave me a deeper appreciation and understanding of myself.

The morning of auditions I awoke with the special feeling that my dreams were soon to be reality. As if in agreement, the majestic blue sky exuded its immense beauty and elevated my spirits to a higher level. On the drive, my spirits were boosted further as the radio station that had originally advertised the auditions played my request.

From the moment I arrived I knew I belonged. The gym was packed with talented male and female dancers. Filled with excitement and anticipation I approached the registration table to turn in my headshot and resume. Stretching, I talked with other dancers. Our enthusiasm fused, and in turn pumped us up.

The first round of the day was a memorable experience. People of all styles and backgrounds took the floor. The vibe was intense, positive, and strong. In groups, we performed combinations across the floor as everyone cheered each other on. Unfortunately, it ended too soon. First cuts were made and the crowd was significantly reduced.

 Next step, second dance.   Longer and a bit more technical than the first one. One hundred moved as one, in an awe-inspiring dance. Never in my life had I been involved in such an invigorating experience, like a symphony of movement that creates the sweetest of sounds. Another cut and again the crowd was considerably decreased. Yet the vibe stayed intense.

We had a few minutes before we learned the last dance and that's when I met Samantha. She asked me what time it was; and when I looked at her I was greeted by the friendliest eyes.   Samantha's skin was the color of cinnamon, as was her hair. Endowed with a perfectly toned body and a gorgeous smile, she was simply beautiful. Her energy was rejuvenating. Even though my body was crying out in fatigue, she gave me the strength to go on. Together we hit the floor ready to master the final routine.

The competition was whittled down to just a quarter of what it originally was. The air was charged with nervous energy, yet so alive. We danced with all our hearts. Pulling everything inside out, and into each move. And then again, dancers were cut.

A freestyle round completed the dance phase of the auditions. Each dancer strived to display a distinct style that showed her uniqueness. We were fierce, on fire, working it for each other and for ourselves.

After the last dance cut, private interviews were conducted and then the first ever M-Squad was selected. Both Samantha and I were chosen! But the best seemed yet to come...

Practices were awesome. Like pieces of a puzzle, we seemed to come together no matter how we were placed. Everyone worked hard and we motivated each other to learn new skills. Our coaches became our best friends, with whom we could share anything and everything. We couldn't wait for our first performance.

However, Samantha Rae never got that chance to revel in our hard-earned success. Called by MTV to dance on their new show the "Global Groove", she headed down to Miami to catch a plane to the Bahamas. On her drive towards her big chance at stardom, she was killed in a car accident.

It's hard to understand why and how something like that can happen. How can someone so beautiful just dance away from this great Earth? Why was she chosen? These are questions that can never be answered.

I feel her spirit when I perform--when the stars are shining bright, and when I lose sight of my own meaning here in this world. I was blessed with the opportunity to have danced with this angel. May her soul dance on forever ... as it does in the hearts of the Orlando Miracle M-Squad.

Karey Autumn Savino

Make Your Own Music

If we can think, feel, and move, we can dance. ~**Margaret N. H'Doubler**

In Rockdale, Texas, on New Year's Day of 1971, Emily Clark was born. At the time, no one knew that this New Year's baby would truly become a role model to celebrate ...

In April 1992, Emily set her dreams on becoming a Dallas Cowboys Cheerleader. She competed in a grueling audition with over 1,000 candidates from across the United States to become one of America's Sweethearts.

During the competition, Emily learned and executed choreographed routines, displayed high kicks and jump splits, and exerted outstanding showmanship, energy, and enthusiasm. She was also evaluated on figure, appearance, and was graded on a written test concerning current events and the history of the Dallas Cowboys.

It wasn't until Emily had her personal interview with Dallas Cowboys Cheerleaders Director, Kelli McGonagill Finglass, that her special need was revealed. **Emily Clark had been deaf since childhood.**

Along with thirty-nine other talented ladies, Emily made the Dallas Cowboys Cheerleaders 1992 Training Camp. However, Emily was not expected to survive the final cuts due to the nature of instruction and performance requiring such intense use of music and hearing skills.

Emily did, however, prove everybody wrong!

By paying close attention to the choreographer Judy Trammell, reading lips, and feeling the rhythmic vibrations on the floor, she was able to perform as well as the other 39 candidates. She received her uniform and became an official member of the squad.

Emily Clark faced her real challenge inside the Texas Stadium at her first football game. There were neither lips to read nor any vibrations to feel from the floor due to the stadium's enormous size. As the announcer introduced the new Dallas Cowboys Cheerleaders, Emily and 39 other Cheerleaders pranced onto midfield. Performing beautifully, they perfectly executed their time-honored kickline and jump splits. To no surprise, they brought the crowd to a roaring standing ovation.

Emily's success didn't stop at Texas Stadium. She performed in every home game, made appearances all over the country, and traveled with the team to Tokyo, Japan for the American Bowl. The pinnacle of her successful career was undoubtedly dancing with her Cheerleaders at Super Bowl XXVII.

The Cowboys were not the only ones victorious that day. Emily is a pioneer for women all over the country who never get the chance to 'hear the music,' yet can dance their way to success. Cheers to Emily Clark for creating her own life's music!

Kelli McGonagill Finglass

center stage

You become one with the music, the lights,
and the collective spirit of the audience."

Contributors' Bios

Mary Ahrenholtz, *Destiny.*
Mary started off her cheer career as a cheerleader for Nebraska Christian College in Norfolk, Nebraska. She served as co-captain her second year on the team. Since 1997, she has taken an especially active role in the cheer world, coaching the Harlan Community Middle School Cheerleaders and participating as a member of the Iowa Cheerleader Coaches Association.

Courtney Andreone, *Give It Your All.*
Courtney is currently a junior at Carmel High School. She is a member of the Carmel All-Star Competitive Dance Squad. For the past two years, she has danced as part of a team. Throughout her junior high and freshman high school years, Courtney cheered on competitive squads. Her freshman team took 2nd in the Indiana State Contest.

Wendy Andry, *C-H-E-E-R-L-E-A-D-E-R-S.*
Wendy has cheered for the past five years. As a sophomore at West Aurora High School in Illinois, she led her squad as captain. That same year she was chosen as a UCA All Star. Wendy has cheered for both football and basketball. Although she is not currently cheering her senior year in high school, she hopes to cheer at Bethel next year.

Sheila Angalet, *Magic Pills.*
Sheila has been an active participant in the dance realm for over twenty years. She graduated from Rutgers University with a BA in Dance. She is a former professional dancer and a children's theatre actress. Since 1976, she has created and instructed a variety of programs in movement, dance, tumbling and cheer. She has coached an All-Star Youth team and is currently the coach for the Metuchen Pop Warner Midget Cheerleader team and for the Metuchen High School cheer team as well.

Peggy Auriene, *Love, Tori.*
Peggy's love for cheerleading stemmed from her participation in high school gymnastics. She has assisted the coach for her own daughter's high school cheer team. For two years, Peggy worked as the assistant coach for a Pop Warner traveling competitive cheer team. Although the team never made it to Nationals, Peggy is very proud of their third and fourth place rankings.

Victoria Balun, *Hit It!*
Victoria has been a cheerleader for the past seven years in Pacific Grove, California. As a sophomore she captained her cheer team and again led the varsity team her senior year. USA selected her twice to their All Star distinction and she was also nominated as an All American. Victoria has spiced up her high school cheer career by participating in the Pro Bowl in Honolulu, Hawaii.

Darla S. Bandt, *So What?*

Cheyenne Barr, *Can't Breathe.*
Cheyenne has been on winterguard and colorguard her entire high school career. Although colorguard and winterguard cannot be defined as cheerleading or precision dancing, the two activities are as integral to a school's spirit as the other spirit sports.

Emily Blacksmith, *Dance.*
Emily danced thirteen years of her life. Currently she is a three-year member of her high school drill team, the award-winning Deer Park Deer Escorts. Last year, her team placed 2nd at a national competition. At another competition, the team was bestowed the award for "Best in Class". As a senior, she teaches a dance class at Deer Park High.

Jamie Bond, *Refreshing Innocence.*

Nocona "Nicci" Boots, *Cheerleaders Are Dumb!*
Nicci cheered for two years on the varsity squad at Mullen High School in Nebraska. Her senior year she led the squad as a co-captain.

Idris Boyer, *Stung.*
Along with five other guys, Idris cheered his senior year of high school. From there, he went on to cheer for the University of Connecticut for two years. This past year, he and his team placed 3rd in the small co-ed division at the UCA National Competition. Idris is a member of the UCA Staff Northeast.

Karin Burk, *With A Smile On My Face.*
Karin has spent thirteen valuable years dancing at the Diane Cole Johnson School of Dance. She also spent four years of her life on the Rangerettes Drill Team at the Jesuit College Preparatory. Karin was a member of the inaugural team. Her sophomore year she served as Chaplin. Her senior year she was chosen for the "All American Marching Award" at camp, an honor bestowed annually to two marchers. Karin is currently a member and a choreographer of the inaugural Austin College Aussies.

Shannon Cajayon-O'Toole, *Pyramid.*
Shannon's cheer career took off during her teen years when she cheered for both her high school and all-star cheer teams. From 1995-1997 she cheered at the University of North Texas. In 1997 she and a stunt partner, Tyler McEowen, took 3rd place at the Partner Stunt Championship. For six years she has been a member of the NCA staff. Currently she and her husband Joe are the coaches and program co-directors of Cypress Academy Cheer All-Stars.

Madison Carlton, *Life As A Cheerleader.*
Madison is in her second year of her cheer career. Madison got her start as a gymnast. After participating in gymnastics for three and a half years, she went on to cheer on the eighth grade team. Her team has taken home the Camp Champion Trophy for two years running. Madison thinks cheering is awesome and plans to cheer *at least* through high school.

Rachel Carpenter, *Whirlwind of Courage.*
Rachel attended St. Michael's High School in Santa Fe, New Mexico and was a member of their dance team. For two and half years, she dedicated everything she had to that passionate team and its members. Rachel was one of the team's main choreographers. Their team took the state championship trophy home five years in a row. They have also been named National Champs as well. Rachel attributes the success of the squad to Lydia Sanchez—their coach, mentor and their spirit. Rachel is now in college but will consider herself a part of that special family forever!

Linda Rae Chappell, *The Thank You Poem*; *Good Bye From Your Coaches*; *What Will They Remember?* and *Called to Greatness.*
Linda is the Spirit Coordinator at William Jewell College in Liberty, Missouri. She directs a program consisting of sixty cheerleaders, dancers and mascots. Since 1967, Linda has played a most active part in the spirit world—coaching, teaching, and judging cheerleaders. She is the author of many books, including Coaching Cheerleading Successfully, published by Human Kinetics. She has also directed a number of instructional videos and is the former consultant to the National Federation of State High School Association regarding videos of safety rules. She is the former owner/president if Dynamic Cheerleaders Association, which conducted camps for twenty-two years in thirty states. Linda Rae is also the former director of the Kansas City Chiefs NFL Co-ed Cheerleading Squad. Although self-proclaimed as older than dirt, Linda plans on being an active participant in the spirit world for many more years to come.

Cindy Clough, *Soul Mates.*
Cindy is the Executive Director of Just For Kix Dance Camps and Children's Program in 100 communities, annually involving 12,000 children. She is the co-owner of Just For Kix Dance Etc. mail

order catalog and JFK manufacturing. She has been the Head Coach of the Brainerd High School Kixters for the past 25years, winning a National High Kick Championship, 8 state titles, and 8 runner-up titles. She is the co-founder of the Minnesota Association of Dance Teams, past President of the Minnesota Association. Cindy has choreographed fifteen major Collegiate Bowl half-time shows. She has been honored and inducted into the Minnesota Dance Team Coaches Hall of Fame, the Brainerd High School Hall of Fame, the *Let's Cheer Magazine* Hall of Fame, and the North Dakota Drill Team Association Hall of Fame. She has been voted the "Minnesota Dance Coach of the Year" by her peers in 1987 and again in 1999. She has also been voted and recognized as one of the 2000's top 5 directors in the Midwest. Currently she serves on the Minnesota State High School League Advisory Board, the *In Motion* Advisory Board, and the *Dance Spirit* Advisory Board. This mother of three is also the author of a dance and drill coaches' manual.

Carly Colao, *First Place.*

Carly has been involved in cheerleading for ten years. She cheered for her high school for one year. That year her team clinched a COA National title. Following high school, Carly cheered on the Senior All-Star Team at Pyramids Cheer and Dance in California. Her all-star team ranked nationally at both NCA and USA venues. Later, on the College All-Star Team, she and her team took honors at both America's Best and NCA. She has been individually honored as the "Best All Around" for two years running. You can now find Carly on the cover of *Cheermix 12.* A student at San Francisco State, she can still be seen cheering on Pyramid's College All-Star Team and coaching the Senior Team. Carly can't even begin to imagine a life without cheer.

Jennifer Coon, *Let Go.*

For thirteen years, Jennifer has spent her life dancing. She was a varsity cheerleader for four years. Her high school team took home the state titles both her junior and senior years.

Amie Jo Crace, *The Big Day.*

Amie's stint as a cheerleader has spanned most of her life. She started off her cheer career as a flag football cheerleader, cheered through middle school and high school and cheered for a year at Ohio University. She has been a part of a state champion team for four years, and a member of a national champion team for two. Since college, Amie has gone on to coach a middle school and an all-star team. Amie is an all-around athlete—having taken jazz and tap for fourteen years and having taught gymnastics for three.

Jeremy Cramm, *Trust.*

Jeremy was a varsity cheerleader for four years at Southern Illinois University. He captained for two of those four years. After graduating with a degree in Exercise Science, he coached the SIU cheer team for a year. He has also been a summer camp instructor for both ICA/WCA and COA. Jeremy is currently employed at COA and has been the Staffing Coordinator and Competition Director. In his free time, he judges competitions and tryouts.

Erin J. Cullen, *I Am.*

Erin's passion for dance sparked at the age of six, when she started taking dancing and skating lessons. During her early adolescence, she took a brief break from the world of dance to pursue the adventures of being a tomboy. She cheered as an eighth grader at her middle school and continued to cheer her first two years in high school. As a cheerleader, she was nominated by NCA both her freshman and sophomore years. Her junior year, she rediscovered her true passion and returned to dance. She became a member of Maine East High School's pom team, the Demon Squad. Her second year on the squad, she led the non-coached squad as a captain. A second-place rating for their UDA Home Routine Competition highlighted her year and secured the team a bid for Nationals. After graduating from Northern Illinois University, Erin has returned to her Alma Mater, Maine East, only now as a coach. She is the assistant varsity coach for the Demon Squad, the 2000 Halftime Illinois State Championship Dance Team. For Erin, true passion always prevails, never surrenders.

Brandy Daimwood, *Making It Big.*

Brandy has danced for twenty years—having trained for fourteen and danced professionally for six. Before dancing for the Orlando Magic, Brandy cheered on her high school cheer team for three years. She then danced for the Orlando Magic for five years, captaining every season but her first. Besides dancing professionally, Brandy spent four years teaching dance classes at the Colby Center for Dance and Performing Arts in Maitland, Florida. Currently Brandy does independent contract work for a number of production companies—including Harddrive Productions and Eventions w/ Dance FX, to name a few.

Shannon Daley, *Last Game.*

Shannon cheered the Towanda Black Knights on for all four years of high school. She cheered on the varsity level for all four seasons of football and wrestling. On the football cheer team, she served as co-captain for two years and captain for the other two. On the wrestling cheer team she served as captain for three. Shannon was bestowed "The All American Cheerleader Award 1998-1999", the Towanda Booster Club Award in 1997, 1998, and 1999 and was honored with the "Diane Roof Memorial Award 2000", an award given to the senior cheerleader on the team with the most motivation, spirit and dedication.

Kelly Dalton, *I Am A Dancer.*

Kelly has danced and tumbled competitively for thirteen years. For four of those years, she danced for the varsity dance team at Antioch High School in Illinois. She co-captained her junior year and headed the team her senior year as captain. Her team won the IDTA State Championship in 2000 in the Class AAA Kick Division. Through Showstoppers Camps of America, Kelly has had the pleasure of performing at the Magic Kingdom and at a pre-season Chicago Bears game. She currently works as a summer camp instructor for Showstoppers Camps of America. You can also find Kelly dancing for the Legend Dance Company, a student-run company at the University of Illinois.

Jeane DeRosa, *#1.*

The cheerleading "bug" bit Jeane at the tender age of four. After spending eight years as a youth cheerleader, she joined her coach and team on a venture to a national competition where they placed third. Jeanne went on to cheer for five years with the Space Coast Challengers, an all-star cheerleading team. In 1995, she and a teammate became the first all-girl twosome to clinch the Florida State Partner-Stunt title. She cheered for Merritt Island High School Varsity Team and led the team her senior year. Jeane wrote her poem, *#1,* during her senior year to inspire her fellow teammates before their state competition. After graduating from high school, she continued her cheer career at Florida State University, her team winning an NCA National Championship. She now cheers for an adult team with the Space Coast Challengers. Jeane also enjoys helping local all-star and high school teams.

Deana Ellison, *Recover.*

After having cheered five years on the Council Rock High School Team, Deana has coached both a Pop Warner Pee-Wee Competitive squad and the Pennsbury High School JV team. Her JV team has been honored a number of times by numerous competitive venues—placing third at the American Open in 1999 and coming home as UCA Camp Champs for four years running. Deana also teaches gymnastics at two local Pennsylvania gyms.

Brynn Erickson, *Baby, I'm A Star.*

One of Brynn's most memorable performances was dancing with the Richfield Tapaires at Walt Disney World. Brynn danced for Richfield High School all four years of attendance—her first year on the JV team and the other three on Varsity. She earned five letters while on the Varsity team and served as the secretary her junior and senior year.

Tyson Ferguson, *Never Give Up.*

Tyson cheered at Michigan State University for three years and at Duke University for one. He has choreographed numerous routines for many competitive high school teams and he coached the U.S. Cheer Team for their Brazil tour. Currently Tyson is the cheer coach at Duke University.

Kelli McGonagill Finglass, *Make Your Own Music*.

As director of the Dallas Cowboy Cheerleaders, Kelli is an internationally recognized leader and trendsetter of the NFL. From the Philippines to the Persian Gulf, she has been representing the Dallas Cowboys since 1984. After cheering for the Cowboys for four years, she was the first cheerleader in history that did not have to re-audition but was selected back automatically by the director for a fifth season. Following her cheerleading career, she was hired as Assistant Director to the DCC. For the past ten years, Kelli has been the director. She is solely responsible for the success and the growth of the most famous cheerleaders in the world. Kelli now makes personal appearances and speeches worldwide. She has also hosted the nationally televised NFL Catalogue Show. Kelli was the first to produce a swimsuit calendar video which is now distributed nationally. Kelli is also the founder and mastermind of DCC Productions, a sports entertainment and special events production company that creates half-time extravaganzas for not only the DCC, but also for the IHL, CBA, and the NCAA.

Amy Fitch, *Here Lady*.

Amy's high school coach inspired her to continue cheerleading. After graduating from high school, Amy went on to coach a high school team herself for four years. During those four years, her team placed first at many competitions. Prior to becoming a pro cheerleader, Amy cheered for a semi-pro team in New Hampshire. She is currently a New England Patriots Cheerleader, and has cheered for them for four years. As a Patriots Cheerleader, Amy has traveled to Mexico City for the American Bowl, and has been featured in the Pro Cheerleader calendar.

Sarah Kingsley Foley, *Imagine*.

Sarah's piece, *Imagine*, was originally written as a visualization exercise for her sports psychology class at Sweet Briar College. Hampden-Sydney College unfortunately lost the fore-mentioned NCAA championship game by one point in triple overtime. Nevertheless Sarah maintains that the game was one of the best in her cheer career. Before cheering for H-SC, Sarah cheered at Fort Morgan High School, at Sweet Briar College, and on the Cheer Virginia Open Team. She founded and volunteered the Sweet Briar/H-SC cheer squad. She has been an instructor for both Cheer LTD and for Cheer Virginia. She is a member, the webmaster and an ex-board member for the Virginia Cheer Coaches Association. Sarah currently coaches at Toana Middle School and at the College of William and Mary.

Brittany Geragotelis, *Ready to Face the World*.

Brittany cheered for three years on the acclaimed Oak Harbor High School team in Washington. Since graduating from high school five years ago, Brittany has gone on to cheer for one year at Washington University and is currently a summer camp instructor for NCA. She has also coached a high school cheer squad for two years and a high school dance team for one. Brittany's talents run many as she freelances for ***American Cheerleader*** and their sister publication, ***Dance Spirit***.

Gina Giannakopoulos, *Heart and Soul*.

Gina discovered her passion for dance at an early age when she began dancing for church functions. She started her spirit career as a cheerleader in junior high and went on to cheer her first year at Maine East High School in Illinois. She served as the co-captain on her freshman team with Allison Kaye. Her sophomore year she switched from cheerleading to dancing for the Demon Squad, Maine East's precision dance/drill team. Her first year on the team, they were crowned Halftime Illinois State Champs in the Ensemble Division and took several first places at other venues. Gina is currently the head captain of the team. Her co-captain, is incidentally the same individual who co-captained with her on the freshman cheer squad! Gina has always been an asset to the squad—serving as Treasurer her junior year and being voted "Most Responsible" for two years.

Julie L. Grogan, *As Good As It Gets*.

Julie has twenty years of cheer and dance experience under her belt. Julie is currently the Head Dance Choreographer for JAMZ Cheer and Dance. She is also the Production Director for their events. In the past, Julie has coached a championship collegiate dance team and has choreographed many routines for major bowl games and for Pro and University half-time shows. As a college student, she danced for the 9-time national championship University of Memphis Pom Squad. After a successful stint in Memphis, Julie went on to dance and cheer for three years as an Oakland Raiderette. In 1998 she was voted as Raiderette of the Year. One of her favorite experiences as a Raiderette was dancing at the Pro Bowl in Hawaii.

Brooke Gruetzner, *One Last Time*.

Brooke was a cheer enthusiast for seven years. During her very busy and active years at Marble Falls High School in Texas, Brooke cheered two years on the varsity team. In addition to excelling in her scholastic activities, she was also named an All-American Cheerleader nominee. Her high school cheer team placed fifteenth at NCA Nationals and also placed fourth at America's Best Cheerleading Competition.

Tracie J. Guenette, *Auditions*.

Tracie's poise and leadership skills have allowed her to stand out amongst a many a cheerleader. Tracie cheered for four years at Lincoln Junior/Senior High School, captaining the team during her senior football season. The voted, "Most Spirited Cheerleader" came back to coach the football cheerleading team three years after graduating. While at Rhode Island College, she cheered for Soccer for two years and was a member of the RIC Gymnastics Team for four. In 1993, Tracie was nominated for the N.C.A.A. Woman of the Year. Her senior year she captained the Gymnastics team. Since 1999, Tracie has been a proud cheerleader for the New England Patriots. Following her high school road of valor, she was voted "Most Spirited Cheerleader" for the 1999 New England Patriots Cheerleader team. Tracie has been a contestant in many pageants. In 1998 Tracie was name Miss Rhode Island America.

Jillian Kendall Gray, *Explosion*.

Cheering is a time-honored tradition for Jillian's family. Jillian's grandmother was the first black female to ever cheer on a traditionally all-white high school squad. At a young age, Jillian followed in her grandmother's footsteps. She began cheering at the tender age of eight. She was the captain of her cheer and dance team in her town's Pop Warner program. Cheering for the Freehold Little Giants in New Jersey, she and her team took 2nd place at Nationals. Although Jillian steered away from cheering in high school in order to spend more time studying, she could not contain the spirit within her and served as the President of the Spirit Club her junior and senior year. Jillian is currently a sophomore at Cornell University in Ithaca. Although she no longer cheers, she attributes her sense of self-confidence and her spirit to her cheer coach, Mrs. Pascal.

Michelle Hall, *Cheerleading Is...*(reprinted from *AICMMagazine*)

Michelle is the co-author of the often reprinted *Cheerleading Is...*poem. She and a group of fellow cheerleaders wrote the poem while in eighth grade. Her early success was a sign of greater literary things to come. Michelle is the founder and co-editor of AICM, the web zine for cheerleaders. Michelle began cheering at the age of five. While in middle school, her team took home the North Carolina state title 2 years in a row and placed second in Nationals two years in a row as well. She was selected to the Varsity squad while a sophomore in high school. She captained the team her junior and senior year. Her All-Star team from Raleigh has gone to Nationals thrice, placing in the top ten twice. On a personal note, Michelle is a four-time All-American Cheerleader and has cheered in the Pro Bowl twice.

Haley Hanna, *Reach For the Stars*.

Haley got her spirit start by cheering for a Pee Wee Football Team. She went on to cheer for another two years at Linden Middle School. During her freshman year at Linden High School, Haley was selected to be a member on the Varsity cheer team. She cheered on the team for all of her four years in high school. Her junior and senior years the Linden Cheer Squad was crowned the Michigan Cheer Coaches Association's (MCCA'S) Sideline Cheer (Class B) State Champs. Her senior year they also took first at every competition they participated in.

Susan Maddox Havens, *Lifelong Friendship*.

Presently Susan is the morning show co-host on Dallas/Fort Worth's smooth jazz station, The Oasis at 107.5, delivering news with a fresh local twist. She has been in the broadcast industry for fourteen plus years, primarily as a news anchor, reporter and a nationally televised show host. Susan recently served as the Director of Media Communications for National Spirit Group, drumming up coverage for cheerleading and dance events across the nation. She cheered and danced throughout her junior high and high school years. Her freshman year, she and the Valkeries dance team at Lynbrook High School in CA won a state championship. Having moved to Oregon, she attempted to start a dance team at her new high school. However, the plan fell through and she joined the cheerleading team. No fancy titles, just lots of fun! She is an avid athlete and if she is not working, she can be found at the track or at the gym along with her husband—a true athlete himself and a high school football coach.

Pamela Headridge, *True Champions.*

Pam is a prominent member of the cheer community. For ten years, she has been the head cheer coach at Oak Harbor High School in Washington. Her team was named the "National Team of the Year 1999-2000". As an individual, Pam has been given the "2000 National Federation Interscholastic Spirit Association Coach" Award and was named the "National Coach of the Year 2001-2002". Pam has also proudly earned the "Excellence in Education" Award.

Catherine Frechette Healey, *Lucky Seven.*

Cathe is currently a New England Patriots Cheerleader. She is a five-year veteran of the team. In 1999, she was awarded "Most Dedicated Cheerleader" and in 2000, she was awarded "Most Spirited Cheerleader" by her peers. As a member of the Patriots Cheerleaders, she has traveled to and performed with her teammates at the 1998 American Bowl Game in Mexico and at the 2001 American Bowl Game in Fort Hood, Texas.

Sandy Hinton, *Drill Team Mom.*

Sandy has had a very productive and happy career as the Director of the McLennan Community College Dance Company for the past twenty-five years. Her company was crowned the ADTS National Champs in 1987 and 1988. In 1991, they were named as the ADTS National Kick Champs. This past year, the company was named Collegiate National Champs by both NDA and ADTS in Division II Dance. Sandy is also proud to have had three of her dancers, including her own daughter, chosen as NDA All-Americans.

Danielle M. Johnson, *Making the Most of the New Millennium.*

Danielle cheered and stunted for Central High School for three years. In 1998, her team proudly brought home the Florida State Championship title. Being a serious student as well, Danielle graduated from high school with high honors. Her piece, *Making the Most of the New Millennium*, was her college essay. She is presently a junior at the University of South Florida. She is the Vice President of the Alpha Delta Phi Sorority at her school. Danielle would like to thank her cheer coach Joy Greene for her high expectations, her inspiration and for always believing in her.

Deanna Johnson, *What Drill Team Means.*

Deanna graduated from Albert City-Truesdale Community School, where she was a cheerleader in 1985. Shortly after, Deanna went back to her alma mater to coach the AC-T Drill Team. During her seven years as assistant coach, she and her team earned several championship trophies at the Iowa State Drill Team State Competitions. They also proudly received a number of other high-ranking trophies during that time. Deanna is now the coach for the Buena Vista University Cheerleaders in Storm Lake, Iowa. She is married to an AC-T alum and has three children.

Justyne Johnson, *Forever Faithful.*

Justyne entered the cheer/dance world as a tap dancer. She is now entering her fourth year as a cheerleader for the Chaminade High School Varsity Team.

Doneeta Kallall, *Pazzazz Prayer; The Coach's Room.*

Doneeta's love for drill team stemmed from her high school years as a majorette. Doneeta was a member of the State and National Championship PIASA Indian Drill Team. As a coach, Doneeta has been a member of the Illinois Drill Team Association for fourteen years. She is also a former officer of the organization. She coaches the Civic Memorial High School (Bethalto, Illinois) "Purple Pizzazz" Dance Team and has done so since 1989. The "Pazzazz" are past Regional, South Super-Sectional, and State

Champs for Illinois. Doneeta's daughter Joanna has also coached the team with her for the past eleven years. Doneeta's husband Robert has been inducted to the Illinois Basketball Coaches Association "Hall of Fame". Her son was also the Grad Assistant Basketball Coach at the University of Colorado. They lost him to cancer in 1991.

Allison Kaye, *Best Friend.*
Allison's love for dance is apparent. She and her sister (also an *STS* contributor), Shaina, have been dancing since they could walk. Before becoming involved in cheerleading, she took six years of dance classes, often sharing the spotlight with Shaina. Allison cheered for three years while living in Alabama. As a transfer her freshman year, she captained the freshman cheer squad with Gina Gianakopoulos (another contributor of this book!). Sophomore year, she was selected to the Maine East pom team, the Demon Squad. As a sophomore, junior and a senior she was selected to represent the squad as a UDA All-Star nominee, culminating with her being named a UDA All-Star her senior year. Allison is currently the captain of the 2001-2002 varsity squad.

Shaina Kaye, *The Back Row Club.*
Shaina Kaye has been dancing since she was six years old. At a young age, she was also involved in competitive gymnastics. Before dancing on a team, Shaina cheered for two years. Her cheer team placed 2nd in the Alabama State Competition. During her second year in high school, Shaina switched from cheerleading to dancing and was a member of the Bob Jones Varsity Dance Team. The varsity team won the camp, regional and state championship titles that year. Having since moved to Illinois, Shaina danced with the Maine East Demon Squad her last two years in high school. Her first year on the squad marked the team's first competitive season. The Demon Squad was ecstatic to make it to State. After five short months of being on the team, Shaina was chosen to serve as co-captain of the team. She co-choreographed their state-winning Ensemble routine. She now attends the University of Illinois where she is still active in dance. In the summer, Shaina teaches the "aspiring young dancer" clinic held at Maine East.

Lyndsey Kilpatrick, *A Family Tradition.*
Following in her sisters' footsteps, Lyndsey cheered at Standley Lake High School for four years. Her freshman year she was a member of the freshman squad and was selected to the varsity squad her sophomore year. During her senior year the team took 3rd at Regionals and at State, and also competed on a national level. Lyndsey wants to give a special thanks to her two coaches who worked so hard, took so much pride in their team, and made it all worthwhile.

Angela King-Twitero, *Dedication to A Dream*
Angela's life has revolved around cheerleading since she was a Pop Warner cheerleader as a child. She is presently the owner of Angela King Designs—a costume design and manufacturing company for professional dance teams. Her curriculum vitae is lengthy and accomplished. After cheering four years in high school, she went on to instruct for USA for 5 years. She then cheered for the San Francisco 49ers for 7 years and directed them for five. She is the former Cheerleader Coordinator for the San Diego Charger Girls, the Sacramento Kings and the Golden State Warriors. Angela is also the founding co-director of the NFL Pro Bowl Cheerleaders as well as the choreographer for the NFL American Bowl Halftime shows. Angela has danced in television commercials and on film and has participated in many USO Celebrity Tours throughout Europe and Korea. Always the advocate for the cheer industry, she is a National Spokesperson and has been interviewed on Entertainment Tonight, Extra, and for various other talk shows and conventions.

Bob Kiralfy, *The Coach's REAL Manual, A Cocktail Recipe.*
As founder and chairman of the British Cheerleading Association, Bob has been involved with cheerleading for sixteen years. He has organized numerous regional, national and international competitions, major shows and training camps. He is responsible for the qualification of nearly 3000 British cheerleaders and coaches. He is the author of "The Most Excellent Book of How to Be a Cheerleader". He is the editor of *Cheerleader* magazine and is the webmaster of the BCA website. Bob has also been a pro basketball mascot for nine years.

Sunney Kohlhoss, *Items A Dancer Should Pack.*
  Sunney started dancing at the age of two, taking the usually toddler ballet classes with a very special instructor, Susan Wolfarf. She stuck solely to ballet until DJ Suave' took her, at the age of thirteen, under his wing and transferred her into a hip-hop dancer. Sunney danced for four years with the Glenbrook South Varsity Poms in Illinois. For three of the four years, she was the co-captain. She has also danced with the Chicago-based company, "Hip-Hop Connection" and has worked with "A-Z Entertainment" as an interactive dancer. She is currently a sophomore at the University of Colorado in Boulder and greatly looks forward to starting a hip-hop company.

Ross A Kolodziej, *The Male Cheerleader.*
  Ross cheered his senior year at Blaine High School in Minnesota. During that time, he was also a member of the Cheer Elite All-Star Cheer Team. He went on to cheer for St. Cloud University in Minnesota for five years. The team has competed at the UCA College Nationals for the past two years and has taken 14th and 8th place, respectively. Since 1998, Ross has been an instructor for NCA. Having just completed his fourth year with the company, he is now a Head Instructor. On his downtime from academics, Ross helps local area high school and all-star cheer teams.

Megan Lambart, *Picking Up the Pieces*; *What I Would Give*; *When She Thought No One Was Watching*; *There's A Hole in My Heart.*
  From 1994 to 1999, Megan was a proud member of Valley Lutheran High School's pom pom team. Her freshman and sophomore years ended in disappointment when the team failed to qualify for Mid American Pompon's State Competition. However, everything changed when Melissa Colon became the team's coach. She inspired the team to succeed, resulting in two Mid American PomPon Coed Dance Championships and one state title. Teammates Janelle Sherouse Wilson and Kristen Herzberger further motivated the dance team through their shining examples of determination and excellence. Though Megan has not performed in several years, the privilege of striving for success with those phenomenal women has made Megan the person she is today. She attests to being a pommer—in spirit—for the rest of her life.

Christi Lee, *My Megaphone, Got Spirit?*
  Christi is presently the captain of Stephenson High's Football Cheer Squad. She has cheered on various squads throughout her life—including the Green Forest Baptist Church's CYO Squad. She has cheered for both the football and basketball cheer teams at both Stephenson Middle and High Schools.

Deborah Scioli Logozzo, *For the Dancer.*
  Deborah danced for the Hofstra University Dance Team from 1994-1998. She served as captain her senior year. Upon graduating from Hofstra, Deborah took a job instructing young dancers for UDA at summer camps. Currently she is the head coach for the dance team at her alma mater.

Kate Lospalluto, *The Sky is the Limit!*
  Besides being an avid cheerleader, Kate has been dancing for the past twelve years at the Chatsworth Dance Center in California. Throughout middle school Kate belonged to both the dance team and the cheer squad. Kate cheered her sophomore year through her senior year at Chaminade High School, participating on the competition squad her junior and senior years. Her senior year she led the squad as co-captain. During her productive cheer career, Kate was voted both "Cheerleader of the Year" and "Best All Around".

Fran Lukkarinen, *A Good Experience.*
  The Little Feathers from Keokuk, Iowa are one of the oldest drill teams in the state. Out of their thirty-one years of existence, Fran co-directed the team for sixteen. In her sixteen years, the team took home seventeen state titles, along with numerous 2nd and 3rd place trophies. Fran coached nine of those years with Marilyn, her cohort in *A Good Experience*. Fran has since retired. Although she has moved from Keokuk, Fran did not leave the wonderful memories and friends behind.

Autumn Lyn Marisa, *This Girl Is A Dancer*.

Autumn has been a member of the Penn State Dance Team for the past three years. She is presently a two-year captain of the prestigious team. The Penn State Dance Team performs at all home football and basketball games, as well as several volleyball, soccer, and field hockey games. The team annually attends NDA camp and competes nationally at the NDA Nationals in Florida. Being a part of the dance team has made Autumn feel truly a part of the large university and its time-honored tradition of school spirit. Autumn is most thankful for the friendships that she has formed around a passion and a love for dance.

Crystal Martin, *Drive to Succeed*.

Nikisha McDonald, *Making the Most of It*.

Nikisha had a most illustrious dance career at the Maine East High School as the first four-year dancer on the Demon Squad, the precision dance/drill team. Nikisha served as the Historian her junior year and was voted by her peers as "Best Teammate". Nikisha is now a dancer on the University of Illinois Precision Dance Team.

Holly G. McGraw, *Buck Up!*

Holly has been a dancer for the past fourteen years, two of those years as a dancer on the Silsbee High School Tigerettes Drill Team. The Silsbee Tigerettes have been awarded time and time again for their standards of excellence. Holly, herself, served as the Vice-President of the team and was named "Outstanding Tigerette of the Year".

Angela Mickelson, *Don't Be Afraid To Dance Alone*.

Angela is a dedicated and determined dancer. Before switching to dancing, Angela cheered for seven years. After attending that memorable Just For Kix camp, Angela went back two more times. She was chosen to perform in the Orange Bowl Halftime Show and did so two years in a row. In college, she was a three-year member of the Minnesota State University-Mankato Dance Team. They took the NDA Division II National Championship trophies home in 1999 and in 2000. Angela performed in five musicals while in college. She also attended the American College Dance Festival her senior year and is now in the process of planning the events for National Dance Week 2002. She is currently employed as an Arts Administration consultant for artists and companies.

Natalie Minns, *Passion*.

Natalie's stint as a high school dancer was very exciting and successful. Her freshman year Natalie and her varsity dance team at McIntosh High School won the State Championship in the jazz division. Transferring to Starrs Mill High School, she was chosen to lead the dance team as captain. She was their captain for three years! All three years Natalie was voted the "Most Valuable Dancer" and was chosen as a UDA All-Star for two. Her team took high honors at the Texas State competition each year and was recognized by UDA for their quality.

Laura Mitchell, *Believe*.

Laura has danced her life away. At the age of five she started at a local college and made her way through the elementary, junior high and high school dance teams. As an eighth grader, Laura danced on the Delhi Eaglettes who placed fourth at a State/National competition. As a freshman, Laura belonged to the Oak Hill Juniors. They placed second at Nationals. Currently, she is dancing for the Kick National Champions, the Oak Hill Oakettes. She is a junior on the squad and looks forward to two more successful years. Laura's love for dance does not end on the basketball court, she also dances and sings for productions put on at the College of Mt. St. Joseph in Cincinnati, Ohio.

Alisa J. Monnier, *Taking Chances*.

Mallory Morse, *On Track*.

Before Mallory became a cheerleader, she was a competitive gymnast. Her tumbling background helped her land a spot on the cheer team. She has been cheering for three years and is now in the freshman cheer squad at her school.

Lauren Muckleroy, *Athletes Are...*

Lauren is a mover-and-a-shaker in the spirit world. She cheered for seven years with the all-star Texas Starz and Elite Stars. At Silsbee High, she cheered all four years. She is a three-time American Cheer Power National Cheerleading Champion. As a dancer, she is currently a member of the Beaumont Civic Ballet Company and an instructor at the Marsha Woody Academy of Dance in Beaumont. She is also a coach for the elementary program at Bak Tuk Gymnastics and Tumbling. Lauren choreographs for the Texas Starz and for other surrounding cheerleading squads and individuals. In her spare time, she teaches at the Bela Karolyi's Gymnastic Camps.

Sylvia S. Mullins, *A Cheerleader's Prayer.*

Sylvia is a thirty-year coach. At Therrell High School in Georgia she has coached the Competitive Cheer, the Varsity, and the JV squads. Her dedication and leadership is recognized by many. She is a three-time finalist for the "Youth Coach of the Year." Cheer LTD has chosen her as their "National Cheer Coach of the Year". She is the founder/director of JR TH Spirit, USACF three-time National Champions. She is also on the Coaches Council for ***American Cheerleader Magazine*** and has also been featured in the mag as a finalist for *Why My Coach is the Best.*

Beth C. Newton-Girard, *A Comparison.*

Beth is a role model for all those aspiring to be professional dancers/cheerleaders. Beth started taking dance classes at the age of 5 and began cheering at the age of twelve. She cheered at both East Lyme Middle School and High School. While in high school, she led her JV squad as a freshman and was also the captain of the varsity team her junior and senior years. During this time she was named as a UDA All-Star Cheerleader and an ELHS Respected Athlete. She also received the Eastern Connecticut Conference All Star Cheerleader award her junior and senior years. Beth went on to attend Eastern Connecticut State University and received a degree in dance and a minor in Physical Education. Since college she has been teaching cheerleading and dance to children, judging competitions, and coaching and choreographing state-winning routines for the ECSU Dance Team, the East Lyme High School Cheerleading Team and the University of Connecticut's Dance Team. As a dancer, she has danced for the Semi-Professional CBA Basketball team, the Connecticut Pride and for the NFL New England Patriots Cheerleading Team. She is currently coaching the dance team and teaching dance at Eastern Connecticut State University.

Lindsey Nodgaard, *Teamwork = Victory.*

Lindsey was in a fortunate position to be a part of the first cheerleading 7th grade squad at Maple Grove Junior High School and the inaugural team at her high school. As her story depicts, it was a very successful year! She cheered for both the football and hockey team throughout high school. She was captain of the hockey squad her junior year and captain for the football cheer team her senior year. Her junior year, the squad was voted as the "Superior Squad" at UCA camp, giving them the opportunity to cheer for the Citrus Bowl in Florida. As an individual she was voted "Most Valuable Cheerleader" by her teammates and was also awarded the "UCA All Star" award by the UCA instructors. Lindsey went on to instruct summer camps for UCA. Cheering, chanting, stunting, dancing, laughing, working, falling, and succeeding are just a few of her favorite things.

Inga Ohman, *International Cheer.*

Inga has been a cheerleader since she was eleven years old. She belongs to the Linkoping Lightnings in Sweden. While on the team, she and her team have gone to five regionals, winning four; and have competed at the Swedish Nationals four times, taking second at three of them. Inga is the co-captain of the squad which is comprised of girls between the ages of thirteen and sixteen. She is also busy coaching an all-girls squad comprised of girls between the ages of ten and twelve. They just attended their first competition ever and came in second place.

Debra Renee Olds, *Getting Involved*.

Debra got her start in dance by performing in talent shows. As a freshman in high school, she danced for the drill team, the Silsbee High School Tigerettes. Her sophomore year, however, she decided she could show more of her spirit by becoming the school mascot. She absolutely loved it! She won two spirit sticks at UCA summer camp, was honored as a UCA All-Star, and was selected as the 1999 Camp Champion Mascot.

Barbara J. Overton, *Saving Grace*.

Barbara, "Miss Ovi", as she is so fondly called, led her school in spirit as a Junior Varsity Songleader her sophomore year at Palmdale High in California. Years later, Barbara returned to her alma mater as the coach of all three cheer squads. Barbara has also successfully coached the Wildflower Elementary team, taking the California State Championship trophy and title home in 2000. In recent years she has also coached the Chaminade College Prep team and is now a coach for the Palmdale All-Stars.

Angelina Palmer, *I Am A Funny Girl Who Dances*.

Judy Paluso, *The Coach*.

Since 1975, Judy has taken an active role in sports. At James Whitcomb Riley High School in Indiana she cheered for three years. For fifteen years, she then worked as an Aerobics Instructor for Shapes New Dimensions/Bally's Total Fitness. In 1999, she reentered the spirit world as a cheer coach at Craig Middle School in Indiana. She is currently entering her second year as the coach at Lawrence North High School and will be the head mentor this year.

Melissa Pennell-Kimble, *The True Cheerleader*.

Melissa is St. Louis' most enthusiastic cheerleader! Since 1985, Melissa has dedicated her life to cheering St Louis' teams to victory. She started her cheer career as a Cardinal cheerleader for the Big Red Line. While teaching elementary school, Melissa was selected to the St. Louis Rams Cheerleaders team and led the team as Line Captain for six seasons. As a representative for the Rams, she cheered in the Pro Bowl of 1997 and appeared on ESPN's "Big Game Catch." Melissa managed to catch a 60-pound blue-striped marlin! She again represented the team in 1997 while going on the USO Tour to Japan. In 2000, Melissa donned the cover of the St. Louis Rams Cheerleader Swimsuit Calendar.

Danielle Piccarini, *A Healing Power*.

Dancing has played a significant role in Danielle's life since she was three years old. Danielle started her passionate pursuit at the studio, "Dance Concepts by Suzie" and continued to dance there for twelve years. While at Weymouth High School in Massachusetts, Danielle was a member and later, a captain of the dance team. After high school, she became a summer camp instructor for UDA. Out of the five years that she has worked for UDA, she has been a Head Instructor for three. She has had the privilege of performing at many venues with UDA , including the Macy's Thanksgiving Day Parade, the Jerry Lewis MDA Telethon, and the New Year's Day parade.

R. Scott Poston, *I'll Be Back*.

Scott started off his cheer career at the University of Mobile in Alabama. After cheering there for a year, Scott moved onto the University of Texas El Paso (UTEP) and went on to cheer with their team for 3 years. While on the team, he and his teammates ventured to USA Nationals three times—the first time taking 6th place and placing 2nd two years consecutively. After college, Scott was not content without cheerleading in his life so while living overseas he coached a Youth Services team comprised of 7th and 8th grade girls.

Jeanette Price, *The Champion*.

Jeanette is as much of a spirit enthusiast as her daughter Courtney. She has eight years of training in classical ballet and has taught ballet and jazz for five years. She has also coached the Wichita County High School dance team for five years and the high school's cheer team for two. She has choreographed numerous musicals for the Wichita County High School and for Scott County High School as well.

Melissa Prussing, *I Made It!*

Melissa is an extremely ambitious young woman and it shows! She has been cheering since the age of seven and hasn't stopped since. Melissa cheered through elementary school and through her Pop Warner years, and then moved onto the Hidden Oaks Middle School cheerleading squad. Her middle school squad was the first to compete out of the county. Venturing afar, the team took 3rd at States and 3rd at Nationals. On an individual note, Melissa, captain of her team, was chosen as an NCA All American Cheerleader her 8th grade year. As an All American, she was given the opportunity to dance in the Florida Citrus Bowl Halftime Performance. Now in high school, she is a member of the Martin County High School's cheer team. They already have had a successful beginning to the season, receiving a bid for Nationals at summer camp. In addition to all this, Melissa is a member of the Sr. Prep Team and the 5-girl stunt group for the Treasure Coast All Stars. In only their first season, the stunt team has clinched three national titles. The Sr. Prep Team, not to be outdone, also took the national championship trophy home for their category. If Melissa is not cheering, she is coaching gymnastics at the YMCA Sportsworld in Martin County, Florida. In the near future, Melissa hopes to make the varsity team and then move onto college cheerleading.

Katie Rank, *Once Again.*

Katie has been taking ballet for seven years. She is currently a dancer at Nancy Clarke's School of Dance in Tulsa, Oklahoma. She has been a performer in the Tulsa Ballet's production of **The Nutcracker** for the past four years.

Kristen Rasmussen, *A Dancer's Words of Wisdom.*

Kristen is a senior in high school. She has been dancing for eleven years with Brooklyn Park Dance in Minnesota, taking classes in tap, lyrical, jazz and pointe. For the past three years she has been assisting with a preschool class to gain teaching experience. She also recently began dancing at The Dance Shoppe. In addition to studio dancing, Kristen danced for three years on the high school dance team. Her freshman and sophomore years she was recognized by her peers as the "Most Improved Dancer" and was voted as the "Most Dedicated" her sophomore year. She was elected to the captain position her junior year. During a tumultuous time for the team, Kristen wrote her piece, *A Dancer's Words of Wisdom.* After leading her team her junior year, she decided to not return to the dance team her senior year. She instead focused on Brooklyn Park Dance and The Dance Shoppe.

Heather Ransom, *Perfection.*

Heather's saga with dance and cheer goes back to early childhood. Heather has been dancing for fifteen years. Currently she is with The Dance Pointe on a two-year ballet scholarship. Besides studio dancing, Heather has been cheering for eleven years. Heather cheered for the Williamsville Junior Football League and competition team. The team did very well, winning 1st place at the University of Buffalo Spirit Challenge and taking 2nd place at the Festival of Lights competition at Niagara. At Williamsville South High School, Heather served as both JV captain and Varsity captain. She was chosen as a three-time NCA All American and a UCA All-Star. As a dancer and as a cheerleader, Heather was fortunate enough to dance and cheer at the UCA/UDA Thanksgiving Parades.

Melissa Hague Reh, *Goodbye.*

Melissa began her dance career on the floors of Kim Kalla's Studio of Dance in Lake Villa, IL. During her thirteen-year training, she won regional and national awards, titles and scholarships. She received additional training in Hollywood and New York City. Upon starting high school, Melissa joined the Antioch Community High School Pom Pons. She danced for four years with the team and led the squad as Captain her senior year. She was voted the 1997 ACHS Poms MVP and was selected as the 2nd runner up for the 1997 Showstopper of the Week at Showstoppers Camps of America. Her team competed on an IDTA state level in Novelty, Pom, Production, Aerobic Funk, and Dance. In 1997, she led the team to a Halftime Illinois Championship. After her high school pom career came to a close, Melissa went on to instruct and choreograph for Showstopper Camps of America for three seasons. At the University of Illinois, she danced and choreographed for the Legend Dance Company. She has also arranged dance routines for several high school and studio groups and has judged state contests. Currently, Melissa is studying for her masters in the Physical Therapy Program at the University of Wisconsin-La Crosse.

Amy Reiter, *Chubby Girl with Pink Glasses*.

Amy currently teaches the fifth grade and coaches a junior high cheerleading squad. Amy has been cheering for some time, having cheered for the St. Louis Rams for four years. While on the cheerleading team, she cheered for the 2000 Super Bowl and performed at many different military bases. Cheering for the St. Louis Rams has given her the gift of life-long friendships.

Heather Reneau, *It Keeps Me Going*.

Heather was a member of the Silsbee Tigerettes from 1996-2000. The Tigerettes won numerous awards including 2nd place at the American's Galviston Festival and 5th place in Pom at the MA's National Championship. On an individual note, over the years, Heather has served as the Historian, Treasurer and the President.

Kate Robison, *There is No "I" in TEAM*.

Kate has dedicated a big part of her life to cheerleading. She was a cheerleader for five years with the Elk Grove Jr. Herd, a Pop Warner team. During her third year on the Jr. Herds, she and her team took won the national title at the USA's Jr. Nationals. She was also selected to cheer on the league's all-star team, an honor bestowed upon the top four cheerleaders from each Pop Warner team. In more recent years, Kate has cheered for the All Star Club Spirit Rockets, which consistently placed in the top three of every competition they cheered at. Currently she is on the 720 All Stars, a Pyramids team. They are a strong team and Kate is confident that they will fare well. She would like to dedicate her poem to her dear friend and coach, D.C., who tragically died recently.

Ali Ropes, *'Twas the Night Before Competition*.

Michelle Rutherfurd, *Daily Therapy*.

Michelle began her spirit career as a member of the Pep Club at Holy Child Middle School. She later became a cheerleader on the Varsity St. Pius X High School Team. She has been a member of the cheer team for the last four years and has led the team for two of those years as Captain. She is a two-time nominee for "All American Cheerleader". Michelle hopes to cheer in college and would love to coach her alma mater cheerleading squad.

Lisa Kubinski Saline, *I Can Do This!*

Lisa is the founder and president of United Performing Association, Inc. Her history with dance and cheerleading dates back thirty-three years, with fourteen years of studio instruction and competition. Her senior year in high school, Lisa was awarded the "Miss Teen of Minnesota" title, a scholastic and talent recognition program. Lisa was selected for the original 36 NFL Minnesota Vikings Professional Cheer team from 600 candidates. She spent four years on the team and traveled to Sweden with the Vikings organization. During that time, Lisa was also coaching the St. Cloud State University Cheerleaders and eventually led them to the NCA Collegiate Cheer Championships in Dallas, where they finished sixth nationally. She is the cofounder and director of the first ever, National Hockey League Professional cheer/dance team for the Minnesota North Star Electric Stars. Lisa has directed/coordinated Bowl game half-time shows, performances on cruise ships and several performances at Walt Disney World. She is a popular lecturer and teacher, and serves on numerous judging panels from state to international levels. She is the founder of the Americup in Minneapolis, the National Coaches Conference in Las Vegas, the International Cup of the Americas in Acapulco and the UPA All Stars Performance Tours. She developed the UPA Judges Certification Program is a writer for several dance/drill and cheer publications, including *American Cheerleader*, *Dance Spirit*, *In Motion*, *Kickline* and the *Cheering Review*. In addition to all this, she is married to her high school sweetheart and has a six-year old son.

Karey Autumn Savino, *Last Dance*.

Karey is an enthusiastic dancer. In five seasons, she has danced in over 80 Orlando Magic and 50 Orlando Miracle home games, the 2000 WNBA All-Star tour and the 2001 WNBA All Star game. She has appeared in local and national television commercials and several Magic Magazine issues. During her two seasons on the Orlando Magic dance team and her three seasons on the Orlando Miracle M-Squad, she often assisted with on-court promotions, conducted radio interviews, attended over 100 community events, and has participated in numerous workshops and camps. She was the Orlando Magic Team leader for one year and the Orlando Miracle M-Squad Team Captain for two. In her downtime, Karey has also danced for several production companies, has taught at several camps and local studios, and has modeled for the NFL 2002 John Madden video game, for the Eastbay Catalog, and for Buggirl Clothing.

Sarah Scoggins, *C-H-E-E-R-L-E-A-D-E-R-S.*
       Sarah cheered for three years in Silsbee, Texas. She is presently not a cheerleader but is still a cheerleader at heart. She chose to give up cheerleading to pursue her musical interests, but still loves the sport!

Ronda Slaughter, *Pure Inspiration.*

Linda Michelle Smith, *Break A Leg!*
       Dance and cheerleading have always played an important part in Linda's life. Her dance instruction began at the age of three, and she continues to both take and teach classes to this very day. Her interest in cheerleading began in junior high and continued through both high school and college. She cheered at Quinnipiac University and The University of Hartford. After college, Linda continued her cheerleading career professionally as a four-year veteran of the New England Patriots Cheerleading Squad. Participating in charity events was one of the most rewarding experiences of being a cheerleader. Linda continues to participate in the spirit sphere, judging many competitions and auditions for the University of Connecticut and The University of Hartford cheerleading teams, and the Eastern Connecticut State University Dance Team. She also judges on a high school level as well.

Christine Spata, *The Time of His Life.*
       Chris is Bill's proud mother. While her son danced on the St. Charles Drill Team in Illinois, Chris played an active and important part in the organization as well. She was their historian, publicity person, their photographer, and most importantly, the drill team's #1 fan! As a child, she too danced and enjoyed the other arts as well. She supported both Bill and his sister Melissa in their dance endeavors. To her, there is nothing like the art of dancing—its substance fills a child with self-worth and confidence and challenges them to discover life's endless opportunities.

Melissa Spata, *A Drill Team Prayer.*
       Melissa took eight years of formal training in dance. During those years, she was a member of the Copeland Dance Academy Performing Dance Company. As a member, she won many local and national awards. In high school, she danced for the St. Charles Varsity Drill Team from St. Charles, Illinois. During her two years as a drill team member, she served as a choreographer. Her team took many state honors at the IDTA competitions. Since then she has gone on to teach a preschool dance program and is currently a first grade teacher in Scottsdale Arizona. She hopes to coach an elementary or high school drill team in the future.

Elisabeth Stallard, *Put Yourself In My Cheerleading Shoes.*
       Elisabeth is an outstanding advocate for the sport of cheer. She started off her cheer career as a Rancho Cucamonga Pop Warner cheerleader. All three years as a pop warner cheerleader, she was awarded the Little Scholars Gold Award. Since her start, Elisabeth has cheered for the Spirit Squad at her junior high, has captained her freshman cheer team at Alta Loma High School, has competed for her junior varsity team, and has captained one year on her two-year stint as an Alta Loma Varsity cheerleader. During her senior year she was voted "Most Valuable Cheerleader" and received the "Coaches' Choice" Award. On all the competitive teams she has cheered on, she and her teammates have taken high honors on regional and national levels. Elisabeth has been nominated and awarded the "United States Achievement Award" in 1999, 2000, and 2001. She has also been nominated by NCA for the ***Who's Who Among American High School Students***. On a team level, all the competitive teams that she has participate on has taken high honors on both regional and national levels.

Katie Talkowsky, *Tanvi.*

Before dancing for the Maine East Demon Squad, Katie took dance lessons from the age of three. As a freshman at MEHS in Illinois, Katie joined the school's dance club, Orchesis. Her sophomore year she was selected as a precision dancer for the Demon Squad. Being the team's first year as a competitive squad, they were ecstatic to make it to State. As a junior, Katie was a dancer and a choreographer for the team's Ensemble, which took first at the 2000 Halftime Illinois State Competition. Katie also served as Treasurer for the team her junior year. As a senior, she led the squad as one of three captains. Katie co-choreographed their competitive kick routine, *I Just Wanna be Happy*, which took 2nd at the 2001 state contest. This was extremely fulfilling as it was the first time that the team had competed in the kick category. Before graduating, Katie was voted as Most Respected and Best Choreographer. She now continues living out her passion for dance as a member of Marquette University's dance team, Intensity. During the summers, she teaches the Demon Squad-hosted mini-camp for middle school dancers.

David Tamez, *Homecoming.*

David's journey and adventures with cheerleading is inspiring for all. However, David's awards, titles, and scholarships could not have happened without support of the following people: GOD, Mom and Dad, NCA, Coloma, Buffy, Amy, Alice, Shalea, Susan Waggoner, Holly, David Carr, Katie Branch, David Hartenbower, Brandon Lane, Renee Casey, Linda Froelich, Guy Yates, Dr. Leigh Browning, Erin Kelly, Mr. Ryan, Mr. Harriman, Mr. Worth, the Seminole Independent School District, the entire high school faculty (the best in the state), Dodie Boyd, Tina Benson, Aine Lopez, and all the past, present and future Seminole High School Cheerleaders.

Angela Tancredi, *Dear Coach.*

For ten years, Angela has lived life as a dancer and a cheerleader. As a member of Notre Dame College's cheerleading team, Angela and her teammates were fortunate to win the 1997 Ontario Championship. During her membership, they also took home three first place regional trophies. Angela spent her first year at Queen's University as a University Competitive Cheerleader. The team placed third at the University National Championship in 2000. On an individual level, she was the winning recipient of the Ontario Cheerleading Federation Scholarship program. Currently Angela is a certified Artistic judge in Ontario. As she has for the past five years, Angela choreographs routines for teams across the region.

Carrie Tharp, *Cheer With My Heart.*

Jennifer E. Toman, *Never Give Up.*

Jennifer's cheer and dance history is as successful as it is colorful. For twelve years Jennifer has been a dancer with the championship-winning Carolina Strut in Morehead City, North Carolina. She has cheered for almost as long as she has danced. She cheered for eleven years beginning with the Pop Warner league in Newport, NC. As a pop warner cheerleader, Jennifer was recognized nationally as an All-American Scholar. Her cheer team at Broad Creek Middle School was honored as UCA Camp Champs and as captain of the team, she was selected as a UCA All-Star. At West Carteret High School, Jennifer earned three varsity letters as a cheerleader. With her as its captain, the cheer team won several regional competitions, placed third at the North Carolina State Contest and took second at ECA Nationals. During her senior year, Jennifer was voted as "Most Valuable" cheerleader at the Spirit Express Camp. She was named All-State and received a Scholar Athlete Award. She also received a Scholar Athlete Award all four years of high school for having and maintaining the highest GPA on the cheerleading squad.

Karen Topping, *I Wish...*

Lynette Weaver, *Unexpected Thanks.*

Lynette's influence into the spirit realm runs deep. Before cheering, she was a competitive gymnast for eight years and she danced for five. Since then she has cheered for nine years. She was the captain of her varsity cheer squad in high school. Since leaving high school, she has worked for Universal Cheerleaders Association. A summer camp instructor for six years, she is one of the company's top head instructors in the southern California. She has judged cheer competitions and tryouts, performed in various parades and Bowl halftimes. Currently Lynette is the head coach of a new All-Star Cheer studio, The West

Coast Gymstones, in Bakersfield, California. She coaches both the jr. and sr. all-star teams. She is planning on taking a trip to Taiwan to give cheerleading seminars and demonstrations.

Christina Lee Wells, *A Coach's Pride*.
When Christina was eight years old, she told her mother that she wanted to be a cheerleader. At that time, no one understood her fascination for the sport. She cheered for her middle school and was deeply disappointed when she failed to make the high school cheer team. Her junior year she went out for the inaugural dance team at Anderson County High School and made it. She shortly after discovered her love for dance. Her coach Lori Price and choreographer Danielle Willis did much to nurture her newfound love. After graduating from high school, Christina returned to her alma mater to coach the dance team. She hopes that she can help other young dancers discover and nurture their passion for dance.

Jonna Werner, *No One Knows Like A Dancer Knows*.
Jonna has danced she she was three years old. Her training includes ballet, jazz and pointe. At the tender age of nine, Jonna became a Bloomingdale Bears Cheerleader. She cheered with the team until she was thirteen. While cheering for the Bloomingdale Bears, she cheered with the Trinity Cheer Team, the 1996 Illinois State Champs. Upon entering high school, Jonna returned to her love of dance. She was a member of the JV Lake Park Dance Team her freshman and sophomore year. She also danced for the school's Orchesis her sophomore and junior year. As a senior Jonna's varsity team took home the 2000 state title in the Production category. On a personal note, Jonna had been awarded throughout her high school years with the Orchesis Dance Award, the IDTA "All Star Award" and "ShowStopper Award", and was awarded with the Academic Award for four years.

Stacy Westerman, *We're Doing This For God*.
Stacy didn't start off as a dancer. Stacy got her start as a cheerleader while in the sixth grade. She cheered through middle school and joined the dance team when she started as a freshman at Central High School. She has captained the squad the past three out of four years. As a senior, Stacy was chosen and honored as a UDA All-Star. Being a member of the Bull-ettes has been one of the greatest experiences of her life. She wouldn't trade it for anything else in the whole world.

Susan D. Wiman, *For Kacee*.
Unfortunately, Susan was unable to attend the University of Hawaii on the dance scholarship that she had been granted. But Susan did not let this stifle her passion for the spirit sports. For the past twelve years, she has been coaching cheerleading. In recent years, her team has taken 5th at NCA Nationals, 8th at UCA Nationals, and was crowned National Champions by America's Best. Susan has coached and choreographed many routines for youth recreation squads in the Shreveport, Louisiana area.

Doug Wintermute, *Ups and Downs*.
As past of his duties as Public Information Officer for Kilgore College in Kilgore, Texas, Doug writes articles and takes photographs of the world-famous Kilgore College Rangerettes. He has traveled with the Rangerettes to the Cotton Bowl, the Fiesta Bowl, The 2001 Presidential Inauguration, and the St. Patrick's Day Parade in Dublin, Ireland. He is also a freelance writer, photographer, motivational speaker and songwriter/musician.

Brigette Skye Workman, *Climber*.
Brigette has been cheering for five years. She is currently the co-captain of the Perry High School Varsity Cheerleading Squad. She has also studied dance for nine years. She trains at Encore Dance Studio in Stillwater, Oklahoma and at Heather's School of Dance in Perry, Oklahoma. She is a United States Cheerleader Achievement Award winner.

Jane Yundt, *Her Spirit Lives On*.
Jane cheered at Purdue University from 1976 to 1978. She has organized the 1997,1999 and the 2001 Purdue Cheerleading Reunions. They coincide the reunions with the Homecoming Festivities so to make the most of their everlasting school spirit. Go Boilermakers!

About the Graphic Artist

Erin J. Cullen

Erin received her Bachelor of Fine Arts Degree in Graphic Design from Northern Illinois University in May 2001. From beginning thought to end production, Erin has organized and implemented the design layout for *STS*. She currently maintains a full-time job at a computer software company while also tackling a variety of projects as a freelance designer. In recent months, Erin has returned to her high school Alma Mater as the Assistant Varsity Coach for the Maine East Demon Squad. Lending her design skills to the team, she has helped give new life to both the Varsity and Junior Varsity squad identities. By creating new logos, the teams have been more publically recognized and commended as elite spirit teams. If you are interested in having a logo created for your team, contact Erin at ecullen_sts@hotmail.com.

About the Author/Editor

Sue Ann Kawecki

Sharing the Spirit—for and by cheerleaders, dancers, and coaches is Sue Ann's first book. Sue Ann freelances for many magazines and websites, including **American Cheerleader**, **Dance Spirit**, and **In Motion**. Her many features on the spirit sports can be found on edanz.com, Channelone.com, Cheerhome.com, and Suite 101.com. She also writes for a number of other publications on topics unrelated to dancing and cheering. She is the webmaster of two Spotlight Sites on eteamz.com.

Besides being a spirit writer, Sue Ann is the Head Coach and Team Coordinator for the precision dance teams at Maine East High School in Park Ridge, Illinois. During her three years of coaching, her team, the Demon Squad, has been crowned NDA Midwest Champions, UDA Midwest Champions, Halftime Illinois State Champs, and most recently, the Chitown Challenge/UPA Grand Champions. She is a member of, and is on the board of Halftime Illinois, one of the precision dance/drill associations in Illinois.

Sue Ann is happily married to her husband Billy and is the proud parent of Jami and Jason.

If you have a SPIRIT experience that you would like to share, or would simply like to get in touch with Sue Ann, please contact her at s.kawecki@worldnet.att.net . Be sure to look out for her upcoming website at sharingthespiritonline.com .